D0506016

Advance Praise

"Reading *S.M.I.L.E.* will not just make you a better salesperson, but a better parent, spouse, friend, and person. The lessons told in this business parable are the foundation for a long and successful career in sales and what is needed to save the integrity of the sales industry today."

—Harry Roberts, cofounder of Mattress Firm

"Steve Rigby has written a delightful parable with an important message: When it comes to people and profits, think *both/and*, not *either/or*. The best salespeople know that a focus on *both* relationships *and* results is necessary for success. Read this book, apply Steve's principles, and get your *S.M.I.L.E.* on!"

—Ken Blanchard, coauthor of *The New One Minute Manager*® and *Servant Leadership in Action*

"*S.M.I.L.E.* would be a great addition to any brokerage wanting to adopt a people-first philosophy or for any agent who wants to transform their career. The philosophies and strategies are easy to understand and apply, and I especially liked the complete review at the end of the book. Even if you're only able to adopt one or two of these ideas, your outlook will change enough to elevate your business little by little until you can revisit the book again."

—Debra Hernandez, Director of Professional Development, Texas Association of REALTORS®

"*S.M.I.L.E.* combines a creative storyline that draws you in, with the success stories of real people. This is a must-read for any sales professional looking to take their business to the next level."

—David Osborn, *New York Times* best-selling author of *Wealth Can't Wait* and *Miracle Morning Millionaires*

"Steve Rigby has proven himself to be a great communicator of ideas in real estate and all selling. His strategies outlined in *S.M.I.L.E.* are invaluable for anyone who makes a living in sales. Steve has always been about helping people fulfill their potential. This book shows readers how to do that in a new and delightful way."

—Don Klein, founder and CEO of Chesmar Homes

"*S.M.I.L.E.* gives clear insight into the secrets of listening. When your guests sense you actually care more about their needs than a commission or sale, then and only then can you build a future in sales. Steve takes you on a terrifically fun journey that teaches you how to build relationships and drive business to your door."

—Bob Easter, author of *The 14 Home Selling Secrets*,
Home Buying Power*, and *The Numbers Game

"The key to success in business and in life is the development of caring relationships. Steve Rigby's gem of a book, *S.M.I.L.E.*, offers a blueprint for practicing and growing our emotional intelligence in order that we might be fulfilled in our work world as well as our personal life. You can't go wrong if you find out how to *S.M.I.L.E.*"

—Lynette Sheppard, author of *The Everyday Enneagram*,
A Personality Map for Enhancing
Your Work, Love, and Life...Everyday

"For those who want to thrive in business and in life, there is no better place to start than here. *S.M.I.L.E.* teaches pivotal sales concepts in a unique way that will help readers soar to success. This inspiring, witty, and colorful book is a powerful story on mastering your professional and personal relationships."

—Keith Zars, founder of Keith Zars Pools

"Steve Rigby's *S.M.I.L.E.* is a masterpiece! He provides the simple, specific formula for putting your customer first and being successful in sales. I highly recommend *S.M.I.L.E.*"

—Larry Kendall, author of *Ninja Selling*

"Steve Rigby has made a tremendous impact on our sales team through his 'simple' approach of putting people first. Over the past two years, our company has experienced exponential growth in sales, revenue, and more importantly, relationships. In *S.M.I.L.E.*, Steve captivates his readers by reinforcing the power of a "smile." This book is a must-read, and we are excited to implement the fundamentals of *S.M.I.L.E.* into our everyday lives."

—Steve Louis, Division President, Bella Vista Homes

"*S.M.I.L.E.* is a simple and easy read in its telling but a rich and meaningful one in the way it teaches both seasoned and unseasoned salespeople. I found its concepts relevant and applicable to the work I do with clients and professionals, and I had many "ah ha" moments as I thought about Steve's approach to sales. Steve's care and concern for others and desire to help people obtain the best in their career and life are genuine. I highly recommend this book and the principles Steve presents to any business person."

—Linda Carter, founder of Life's Next Step

"Steve has taken complicated, business-oriented concepts and woven them into a story that simplifies and focuses in on what is truly important and effective in sales. *S.M.I.L.E.* shows us how to treat customers, clients, and people, so we can make it in today's fast-paced world. The key to success in business and in life starts with the principles Steve offers his readers, but this is something that's overlooked at even the best business schools in the country. Apply the concepts in *S.M.I.L.E.* You won't be disappointed in the results and your work and relationships will be better for it."

—Anthony Siela, Managing Member, PSW

"*S.M.I.L.E.* is a must read for those who want to succeed in retail sales in today's crazy world of disruption."

—Charlie Roberts, COO Roberts Brothers
Consulting Group

S.m.i.l.e.

S.m.i.l.e.

How a **People-First Philosophy**
Creates Extraordinary Sales

Steve M. Rigby

GREENLEAF
BOOK GROUP PRESS

Published by Greenleaf Book Group Press
Austin, Texas
www.gbgpress.com

Distributed by Greenleaf Book Group

For ordering information or special discounts for bulk purchases, please contact Greenleaf Book Group at PO Box 91869, Austin, TX 78709, 512.891.6100.

Design and composition by Greenleaf Book Group and Sheila Parr
Cover design by Greenleaf Book Group and Sheila Parr
Cover image © Shutterstock / Hintau Aliaksei
Interior wood sign image ©Shutterstock / Natalia Sheinkin; Owl image ©Shutterstock/Pushkin; Eagle image ©Shutterstock/Yayayoyo; Dove image ©Shutterstock/AKIllustration; Parrot image ©Shutterstock/Teguh Mujiono; Paper Tent image ©Shutterstock/AVS-Images

Publisher's Cataloging-in-Publication data is available.

Print ISBN: 978-1-62634-564-5

eBook ISBN: 978-1-62634-565-2

Part of the Tree Neutral® program, which offsets the number of trees consumed in the production and printing of this book by taking proactive steps, such as planting trees in direct proportion to the number of trees used: www.treeneutral.com

Printed in the United States of America on acid-free paper

18 19 20 21 22 23 24   10 9 8 7 6 5 4 3 2 1

First Edition

For Susan, my wife and soul mate.

And for Rolly Stirman, the mentor who inspired me to be not only a better salesperson but also a better *person*.

Contents

Foreword

As a photographer for *National Geographic*, I have shot thousands of portraits of people from all over the world. Early on in my career, I pushed very hard to make certain I "got the shot." I did get a lot of them, but even more seemed to get away. No, folks didn't literally walk away from me, but often their expressions seemed forced or "pasted on." Slowly, I began to realize that my desire to "get the shot" was getting in the way. I was focusing on the image in the camera, rather than on the living, breathing human being in front of me. My photograph, I realized, was more important than the person.

I changed my focus to make my photography about the person, and after that, everything changed. When I began first connecting with the people I was photographing; when they knew that they, and their stories, were more important than my photographs, well, they opened like flowers. When that happened, it wasn't the light from the outside that lit my images; it was their light from within.

Steve Rigby has discovered this same truth in his life—that light that shines from within us when we put people first. No, he's not a *Geographic* photographer, but he's the most enlightened and most successful salesperson and trainer I've ever met. I say "most successful" because he has achieved what I would call genuine prosperity—wealth combined with a work/life balance that most of us can only dream about. I say "most enlightened" because he not only has a clear vision of what it takes to be successful but also actually lives and shares those principles every day. Steve is a man who truly "walks his talk."

At the heart of Steve's philosophy are values we all aspire to possess: honesty, integrity, decency, character. It's much too easy for these to get lost in the hurly-burly world of sales. "It's just business" rises far too often when these values are called into question. Not for Steve. For Steve, all selling is the *result* of trusting relationships. It's these bedrock values that allow trust to flourish, and the relationships that grow from this trust are the key to real success.

Sounds simple and, on one level, it is. But truly understanding why these values are so important and being able to integrate them into your life every day so they are not just a wish but a habit, well, that's where this book comes in.

S.M.I.L.E. is a new road map. A step-by-step guide which will allow you to see your business and your life from a different perspective. A perspective of service and caring where money is the result, not the goal; where your attitude and actions ignite the inner light in others; where making others smile makes you smile as well.

S.M.I.L.E. is a lens that allows you to see the incredible power of trusting relationships and then gives you the tools to build them.

Now it's time to begin. Turn the page, start the journey, and get ready to *S.M.I.L.E.!*

Dewitt Jones
Photojournalist, film director, author, keynote speaker

Introduction

P ure, profound, and poetic. What a beautiful philosophy by which to live one's life. I concluded my first book on sales with this message. Reflecting on where I am today, it seems an appropriate way to begin this book—also about sales.

Careers can be difficult, particularly those that involve sales. I know. I've sold sawmill equipment and starved. I've sold automobiles and sucked. I've sold real estate and struggled. You noticing a pattern? Hey, at least I was consistent *and* persistent.

Then, I tried selling new homes and succeeded—succeeded beyond my wildest dreams. So what changed? What was different? Why the turnaround?

As corny as it may sound, I learned how to smile. Not the finished version of **S.M.I.L.E.** you hold in your hands but a fragmented version—a version that came to me in bits and pieces, from a variety of sources, spread out over many years. Some came from books I read. Others from sales people I studied. Many came from training I received. And a few, the result of personal experiences. With each sliver I gained more insight into learning *how* to **S.M.I.L.E.**

The joyous journey Sherri Montgomery is about to take you on is not unlike the road I traveled that led me to writing this story. Growing up, I followed the Golden Rule. I was taught to always take the high road with everyone and everything. I focused on serving and caring. I was most fortunate for that early direction.

Unfortunately, much of the knowledge and training I received in my failed attempts at sales focused not on serving and caring but on selling and closing. It took me in another direction—down a different path—one that led me to losing who *I* was. I wasn't proud of what I was becoming. I wasn't pleased with the person I saw in the mirror. I was lost. And I wasn't . . . smiling.

S.M.I.L.E. is dedicated to the sales people in all industries who have lost *their* way. I see them everywhere I shop. I recognize that look on their faces when I'm looking for appliances, clothing, furniture, and bedding. I witness it when I search for automobiles, RVs, insurance, or real estate. I see them struggle, I see them lost, and it pains me. Because *I've* been there, and I don't want *them* to be there another day.

My wish for **S.M.I.L.E.** is simple. It begins with making the life of every sales person less difficult. But it goes far beyond that. Ultimately, it's about making their life one worth celebrating—one that's fulfilling, enriching, and purposeful—personally *and* professionally! I wish to see more . . .

Section 1:
Preparing to S.M.I.L.E.

A Pleasant Surprise

At last the weekend was over, and Sherri was exhausted. She had expected this new career in real estate to be challenging but never imagined it would be this tough. After taking a call from the one family who had purchased from her, she quickly checked her messages before collapsing onto the loveseat under the shade of her back patio.

Watching the blades of the ceiling fan spinning around and around, Sherri was reminded of her efforts the past few months. She had been touring clients around and around and had only the one sale to show for it. And she was convinced that family only bought because they felt sorry for her.

Worse yet, she had few prospects for future sales. As for listings, the only one she had secured was overpriced, but she took it because she needed the exposure. "Maybe I'll get lucky and the market will heat up," Sherri thought. "Then people will be more willing to spend." All she knew for certain was that *she* was spent.

Seeing her reflection in the glass patio door prompted another reflection—her decision to get into real estate. She had considered renewing her teaching certificate after her daughter left for college. Sherri had enjoyed her years in the classroom and felt gratified knowing she'd made a difference in her students' lives. But longing for more, she decided to become a real estate agent, hoping to make a difference financially for her family. "I deserve to be compensated fairly for my hard work and dedication," she stated with conviction.

Six figures was the goal Sherri had set for her first year as an agent. With only one sale in three months, attainment seemed unlikely. Sighing, she leaned back, put her feet on the coffee table, and closed her eyes. It would be hours before her husband would return from a music venue with his buddies. Perhaps some quiet time was what she needed.

Suddenly, an unfamiliar noise disturbed her slumber. Sherri sprang to her feet to discover a parrot perched on the other end of the loveseat. A parrot! It was a stunning bird, both in beauty and stature, easily two feet in height. Its body was a bright yellow with wings and tail feathers a vibrant shade of blue. Curiously enough, it apparently meant her no harm. It just sat there quietly, almost as if it had been invited.

Seeking space to regain her composure, Sherri took a seat in a chair at the end of the coffee table and watched in awe as the magnificent bird calmly looked around, taking everything in. She felt compelled to say something. "Polly want a cracker?" she asked instinctively.

The bird slowly turned in her direction and tilted its head slightly. "I don't mean to disappoint you, ma'am, but my name is not Polly," it calmly replied. "And are you genuinely offering me a cracker, or is this how you greet all parrots?"

Sherri was stunned. Not that the parrot could speak, she expected that. But it seemed to be communicating with her. Again she responded with the familiar question, "Polly . . . want . . . a . . . crack . . . er?"

"Thank you, ma'am," it answered, sounding more human than parrot. "It would be rude not to accept your offer. I would very much like a cracker."

"Well, that won't be a problem . . . I guess. I mean . . . well, I don't know what I mean," Sherri stammered.

"You remind me of a farmer I met who was holding a rope," the parrot stated. "He was so confused, he didn't know whether he had just found the rope or lost a mule."

Sherri was even more dumbfounded. Not only was this parrot talking with her, it was joking, too! She chuckled, feeling a little more comfortable. "I guess I *am* confused. I'm just not used to having a real conversation with a parrot. Can parrots actually communicate with humans?"

"Yes, ma'am, but most folks in your species aren't good conversationalists," it replied with a wink.

"Well, perhaps I am part parrot," she chuckled.

"Who knows, you might be. And I love your sense of humor, ma'am."

"As I do yours, and your manners," Sherri responded. "But you don't have to call me 'ma'am.' I'm not *that* old."

"I assure you my manners have nothing to do with age; they show my respect. My parents taught us that good manners never hurt anybody. Saying 'yes, ma'am' and 'no, ma'am,' and 'please' and 'thank you' weren't an option, Sherri."

"How do you know my name?" she asked with suspicion. "I haven't introduced myself. Are you one of those secret drones that can spy on people?"

"I assure you, Sherri, I'm as real as real can get." Tucking its beak under one wing, the parrot pulled out a small feather and presented it to her. "See if this is real enough for you."

Sherri examined the feather and then moved back to the loveseat. "I'm sorry. I just wasn't sure if I should trust you."

"No need to apologize. After all, we just met. It's important that you trust me, just as I must trust you. Trust is the most important thing in any relationship," the parrot explained. "Now as for how I know your name, I was referred to you by someone you know and trust, someone who really believes in you and wants you to be successful."

"It's my best friend, Charlene, isn't it?" Sherri guessed. "But now that I think about it, she wouldn't do that without giving me a heads up. But my broker would. He's worried I'm not going to make it in real estate. It's him, isn't it?"

"Sherri, at this moment, who sent me is not important. What is important is that we get started off on the right foot. Is that offer for a cracker still on the table, or is it in a box somewhere in a kitchen cabinet?"

Sherri laughed. "I love your quick wit."

"Thank you, ma'am. My folks always told me to keep my wits about me. 'Don't take life so seriously,' they'd say. 'We're not going to get out of it alive anyway!'"

As Sherri nodded in agreement, her cell phone signaled a new text from an agent notifying Sherri that her listing didn't work for her clients. She texted back that she would contact her later. "Now where were we?" she asked, returning her attention to the parrot. "Oh, we were about to head to the kitchen." She put her phone in her pocket and extended her forearm. "May I walk you in?"

"I would be honored," the parrot replied, hopping onto her arm. "By the way, my name is Rolly."

"It's nice to meet you, Rolly," she said with a grin. "Polly . . . Rolly . . . I wasn't far off, was I?"

"Only one letter," Rolly chuckled. "But then close only counts with horseshoes and hand grenades."

Their laughter was interrupted by Sherri's cell phone. She positioned her forearm so Rolly could hop onto the kitchen island and then fumbled in her pocket to answer the call. After a brief conversation, she put away her phone and explained the interruption. "That was Charlene. Along with being my best friend, she's also my hairdresser. She invited my husband, Doug, and me for dinner tomorrow. Which reminds me, I still owe you those crackers."

As she searched the pantry, Rolly responded, "You really don't have to go to any trouble."

"It's not a problem," Sherri assured him. "No problem at all. Now if I could just remember where I put them."

Make Me Feel Important

Rolly took the opportunity to view his surroundings. The spacious kitchen opened to a comfortable great room that was tastefully decorated. Above the fireplace was a portrait of Sherri and her family. Just off the kitchen, an engraved plaque was prominently displayed on a desk area. "I'm admiring your beautiful home," Rolly stated.

"Just disregard the dust," Sherri yelled. Moments later, she shrieked as if she'd discovered gold. "Rolly, do you like Goldfish?"

"I do, Sherri, but I have a hard time catching the little critters. They are too fast and slippery."

"I'm not talking about the swimming kind," she explained. "I'm talking about the cracker kind."

"Yes, I do like those," he said eagerly.

Sherri presented a bowl of Goldfish crackers and a cup of water so Rolly could easily reach them.

He gulped one cracker down. "I appreciate the treat—and the thoughtfulness."

"It's no problem. I'm enjoying your company."

"It's an honor to be here!" Rolly remarked. Glancing toward the great room, he added, "While you were on your treasure hunt, I couldn't help but notice the portrait above your fireplace. Beautiful setting and gorgeous family. Is that recent?"

"Let me think . . . that would have been four years ago when I taught Carly, our baby, during her freshman year in high school. And John David, her older brother, had just started college."

"One big happy family!" Rolly said, admiring the portrait again. "Where are Carly and John David now?"

"Carly is attending a local university and has made the Dean's List! As for our son, he just graduated and is now working at Doug's car dealership."

"Congratulations! You must be proud!" Turning toward the desk area, he continued, "And I love this plaque—especially the message!"

Sherri brought it over for Rolly to examine more closely. Engraved in bold letters were the words

**Education is not the filling of a pail,
but the lighting of a fire!**

Sherri also shared the handwritten note she displayed with the plaque. The message read, "*Thanks for lighting our fire!*" and was followed by dozens of signatures. "The plaque was a gift from my last class. It still brings tears to my eyes."

"I can tell. I would love to have a photo of you holding it to use in my training."

"I can take a picture with my cell phone and print it for you," Sherri offered.

"Thanks, but I'll use mine." Reaching under his left wing, Rolly pulled out his phone. "I had a special sling made that's hidden beneath my feathers."

After posing for Rolly's picture, Sherri placed the plaque and note back on the desk. "So you do training? What kind?"

"Mostly sales, in all sorts of industries."

"And how did you learn that?"

"Years ago I lived with a top trainer for IBM and Dale Carnegie. He practiced on me, and over time, I just picked it up. I was honored to eventually train with him."

"Impressive! You must be really good at it."

"My graduates tell me I have a gift," Rolly answered humbly. "I get numerous referrals and am blessed with a very full calendar." Glancing down at his water, he added, "My cup runneth over, so to speak."

"If you're that busy, I'm surprised your phone hasn't been ringing off the wall, so to speak," she said, sounding skeptical.

Rolly held out his phone so Sherri could read the screen. She counted two missed calls, one voice message, two text messages, and one email. "Has your phone been on mute the entire time you've been here?"

Rolly tucked it away. "I was just being respectful."

"But weren't you afraid you would miss something important—perhaps some new business?"

"At this moment, there's nothing more important to me than *you*," Rolly replied. "Think about it. If I were to take a call while visiting with you or if I simply glance at my phone to check an email or a text message—even for just a moment— what message am I sending you?"

"That whoever or whatever is on your phone is more important than me."

"Precisely! And that is the exact *opposite* of what I want to say. My goal when I'm with you is to make you feel like you're the most important person in my world, period!"

"That makes me feel so special!" Sherri exclaimed. "Have you always treated people that way?"

"I was inspired by Mary Kay Ash, the founder of Mary Kay Cosmetics. She was speaking at a hotel where I was training. On a break, I overheard a reporter ask what the key was to her success. Can you guess what her answer was?"

Sherri considered the possibilities. "Innovative marketing? Product research? Superior business strategy?"

"Those are all plausible, but Ms. Ash attributed her success to something very simple. She pretended that every person she met had a sign hanging around his or her neck. And that sign said . . ."

Make *me* feel important!

"That is simple! And profound!" Sherri cried. Then the lesson of the sign dawned on her. "I feel horrible about the sign you must have thought I saw you wearing. The one that said, 'Make the person contacting Sherri feel more important than Rolly!' I've done that twice already. And the irony is both could have waited until later. Will you forgive me?"

"There's nothing to forgive, Sherri."

"But I didn't mean to be inconsiderate. I just thought I was staying on top of my business—being responsible."

Phone Etiquette

Interesting choice of words," Rolly said. "Instead of being respons-*ible*, imagine how you would feel being respons-*able*. *Able* to respond in a way that's respectful to the person in front of you *and* the person trying to reach you."

"Then everyone would feel important," she concluded. "But how can I make that happen?"

"Go to your ringer setting on your cell phone and read the choices it gives you."

"There's Sound, Vibrate, and Mute."

"From the standpoint of good manners, let's consider how those are mislabeled," Rolly suggested. "The first setting is Sound, which, when you're in the presence of others, would be more aptly labeled 'Rude.'"

"I hate to admit it, but you're right," Sherri agreed.

"Now think about the Mute setting. What could that be labeled to show good manners to the person you're with?"

" 'Respectful' seems appropriate. That's the word you used when you showed me your phone on mute. You said, 'I was just being respectful.'"

"I did. Putting your phone in the Respectful position says, 'I want to make *you* feel important!'—Mary Kay Ash's philosophy."

"I love this!" Sherri exclaimed. "But what if I have clients flying in from out of town and I've told them to call when they arrive? How can I be respectful to them and still be respectful to the person in front of me? I often feel trapped into answering all my calls and messages."

"Maybe that's why they're called 'cell' phones. We feel we're trapped in a cell and can't escape."

"So how do I *free* myself?"

"You simply put your phone in the 'Respectful to Both' position—the Vibrate setting."

"But I still have to check it when it vibrates. Isn't that being rude? So what's the solution?"

People First and Product Second

Do what my brother does."

"Wait a minute. You have a brother?"

"Yes, ma'am. In fact, I have several brothers and sisters. Our parents were real 'love birds.'"

"How sweet, Rolly. But now I feel worse than ever. You've been so interested in learning about my family and making me feel important, whereas I have totally ignored you and your family."

Sherri shook her head. "Looking back, I've done this with my clients, ignoring them as people. On the listing side, I've focused more on the home I'm hoping to list than the person living in it. On the selling side, I've been more focused on the home someone is looking for than the person who's looking for that home."

"You're not the first person in sales who's put the product ahead of the person."

"But I realize now it should be people first and product second. I feel terrible!"

Her eyes welled with tears, so Rolly moved closer. "Don't worry, Sherri. Everything will be fine. If you feel comfortable, let me give you a hug. A hug says 'I understand' in a way words never can or will."

Rolly gently spread his wings. Without hesitation, Sherri—feeling more like she had been talking to her best friend—accepted his embrace. "You're special, Rolly. I see now I've got a lot to learn. Will you help me?"

Learning and Accountability

I would be honored to help you—and *will* help you—with two stipulations."

"I'm all in, Rolly. What are they?"

"For starters, I need you to keep doing what you're already doing. I need you to *want* to learn."

"As a former teacher, I love learning. I aced my real estate exam and excelled at the training from my company."

"That's wonderful! You also noticed the need to make others feel important and to practice better phone manners, which tells me you can readily incorporate new strategies. We just need to make certain you're learning the things that are most important."

"Such as noticing things that are meaningful to me, like my plaque? Or wanting to learn about my family, as you did with the portrait?"

"You have been paying attention!"

"It's easy for a teacher to recognize when she's being taught by example. I admire someone who walks their talk."

"Even if my walk is a little odd?" Rolly asked, strutting back and forth with his head bobbing up and down.

"I think your walk is cute!" she said, defending him. "So what's the second stipulation?"

"Let me answer in a way that will be a daily reminder. Look at your hands and tell me what you notice."

"I notice I really need to paint my nails."

"That's not the answer I expected, but now I know that's a priority to you. So let's try this again: what are your nails a part of?"

"My fingers," she responded sheepishly.

"Correct. And when you were young and learning numbers, how did your fingers help you?"

"I used them to count."

"Yes, you were 'able' to 'count' on them."

"I think I know where you're going!" Sherri chimed in. "You want me to look at my hands every day and remember that I must hold myself acCOUNTable—accountable for applying what I'm learning. Is that it?"

"Exactly! And recognizing that is crucial," Rolly replied. "If you'll do that, we'll both be pleased with the results, as will the person who got us together."

Holding up her hands, she pledged, "You can count on me to hold myself acCOUNTable every day!"

Taking Care of a Problem

Now let's get back to your question about how you can check your vibrating phone without being rude to your guests. To answer that, I'll share a secret I learned from my brother who's been happily married for thirty-five years."

"Parrots get married . . . for thirty-five years?" she asked in amazement. "How long do parrots live?"

"Parrots are monogamous and can marry—and then they're together for the rest of their lives! And we have about the same life expectancy as humans," Rolly explained, touched by Sherri's interest. "Are you pretending to see a different sign hanging from my neck?"

"I'm just holding myself acCOUNTable," she said, wiggling her fingers. "So tell me your brother's secret."

"My brother told me he learned to take care of a problem

before it could *become* a problem. Each night before he and his wife went to their perch, my brother placed two aspirins and a glass of water on her nightstand. When she'd question the purpose of the aspirins—since she didn't have a headache—he'd respond, 'Great, I'm glad we got that out of the way!'"

Sherri almost doubled over laughing. "That's a delightful story!"

"It is, but it also demonstrates the importance of being proactive. So let's consider what you might do with your guests. Within the first few minutes, you could pull out your phone and simply share that you're switching the ringer to Respectful so you can give them your undivided attention."

"How simple, and what a powerful message it sends! And if *I* show that respect to my guests, do you think *they* would be inclined to show the same respect for me? Would they turn *their* ringer to Respectful and offer me *their* full attention?"

"I'd almost guarantee it! So picture the interaction with your guests: no one is a captive to their cell phone."

"That sounds liberating. But what about the situation I posed earlier where you have to leave it on vibrate?"

"I'll bet you could figure out what to say. Care to try?"

Holding her phone, Sherri imagined the conversation. "Mr. and Mrs. Clients, I am so enjoying my time with you that I'm putting my phone on vibrate so I can pay close attention to our conversation." After changing her ringer, she continued. "Usually I switch it to mute, but I'm expecting a call I promised I would take, and I'd like to honor that commitment. I trust you're okay with that."

"I couldn't have said it better myself! Hearing you formulate the ideal response makes me happy."

"Thanks, Rolly," she replied, switching her phone back to mute. "Making you happy puts a smile on my face."

Section 2:
S.M.I.L.E.

The Power of a Smile

I t's interesting you say that because that's actually the reason I'm here—to teach you *how* to **S.M.I.L.E.**," Rolly said.

"To smile? I'm so intrigued that the teacher in me wants to take notes. That way, I can better remember what I'm holding myself acCOUNTable for." Sherri grabbed a pen and notepad from her desk. "Where do we begin?"

"Let's begin by having you draw a curved line horizontally."

"How's this?"

"Perfect. Now draw the same curved line above or below, connecting it with both ends of your first line. What does this image remind you of?"

"It looks a little like a rainbow. Or perhaps an umbrella—without the pole and handle."

"Now look what happens when we change our perspective. Take your pad and rotate it 180 degrees and tell me what you see."

"That's easy, Rolly. It's a smile!"

"And notice how long it took you to recognize it."

"It was instantaneous. The moment I saw it, I knew what it was."

"And what do people usually do when they see someone smiling?"

"Smile back, just as I did when I saw the image."

"Precisely!" Rolly agreed. "Now let's talk about the

significance of this in terms of people's perceptions. Do you feel most people are optimistic or pessimistic?"

"Pessimistic, by far. Most people I know have a 'sky is falling' mentality. They worry a lot and expect the worst. And they tend to focus on the negative aspects of a situation more than on the positive."

"Pessimism is a perspective for many people. Some estimates are as high as seventy-five percent of the population. So do you think pessimists walk around with a big smile on their face? Or"—Rolly used his right foot to turn the image upside down—"with a frown?"

"Oh!" Sherri exclaimed. "At first, I didn't see this as a frown, but I do now. And that's what most people are wearing. They're frowning, not smiling."

"So do you think pessimists would be more likely to feel happy around someone who is frowning or someone who is wearing a smile?"

Sherri turned the image back around so she and Rolly could see the smile. "They would be more likely to feel happy around someone who is smiling. I think people who smile can spread happiness to others."

"I agree. Happy people spread joy throughout the world! And in the business world, we get rewarded for spreading happiness. That's why sales people who smile and make people happy sell more and enjoy much higher incomes. And restaurant servers who smile and make people happy receive bigger tips."

"Come to think of it, Doug and I often drive thirty minutes in traffic to dine at our favorite restaurant. But it's not the restaurant or the food or the prices that attract us. We go there because of our favorite waiter, Rob Lee, and his smile. And even though Doug and I are naturally happy people, we love how good he makes us feel."

"And do you reward Rob for that smile?"

"Absolutely—and generously! We go there only on days when he's there and always ask for him. We refer him to our friends. Now I see why I need to smile more."

Sherri turned the page back around to reveal the frown. "When I'm *not* smiling, I'm *not* selling." She forced a scowl to mirror the image on the page.

"Your day will go the way the corners of your mouth turn," Rolly remarked.

"That's so true! And I get to choose that direction every moment of every day. It's obvious I need to have the right perspective. I need to smile more. Is that what you meant by teaching me to smile?"

"It actually goes beyond that," Rolly explained. "You see, a smile is *what* you do. And that's very important. But I want you to learn the *meaning* of the word 'smile.' The meaning is found in the letters that make up the word."

"So everything I need to learn to turn my real estate career around can be found in the spelling of smile?"

"Not exactly, Sherri. There's a lot that goes into having a successful real estate career or any career involving sales. But in learning to **S.M.I.L.E.**, we'll cover a few of the most important things. I want to make this simple, so we'll only touch on the secrets behind these five letters."

"The simpler, the better, *I* always say." With that Sherri wrote a big *S* on the left side of the next blank page in her notepad and underlined it for emphasis.

$$\underline{S}$$

Section 3:
The *S* in S.M.I.L.E.

SIMPLE

S o let me guess, the *S* stands for smile, right?" Sherri asked.
"The beauty of **S.M.I.L.E.** is that the letters can represent different things to different people. So it can remind you of how important it is to smile," Rolly replied. "But you might want to consider a more relevant term that you *just* said was important to you."

"You mean 'simple'?" Sherri wrote the rest of the letters to form the word. "Why 'simple'?"

<u>S</u>IMPLE

"The word 'simple' is important because people tend to overthink things. Have you heard someone say, 'This isn't rocket science' or 'This isn't brain surgery'? What do these statements mean?"

"Keep it simple—that things aren't that complicated."

"With that in mind, tell me what you learned in your training about selling."

Sherri's mood immediately plummeted. "I learned about

qualifying, demonstrating your product, feature-function-benefit, tie-downs, open-ended questions, and close-ended questions. Then I learned every close from A to Z, literally. Oh, and my ABCs—to Always Be Closing. And as if that wasn't enough, I learned trial closes and objections and how to overcome them. At times, I felt more like I was being trained as a trial lawyer than as a real estate agent."

"And how is all of that working for you, Sherri?"

"Poorly! During the goal-setting session—which I forgot to mention—we were encouraged to set stretch goals, so I set a goal of making six figures my first year. Well, a quarter of the year is gone with only one sale. And though I changed careers to make more money, it felt like the training was *all* about money."

"First off, goals are important. And when appropriate, there's a time and a place those techniques can be useful. But when the focus was *all* business—about making a dollar—did you get the sense it made selling seem a little . . . complicated?"

YOU Are the Most Important Sale

That's an understatement, Rolly. It was overwhelming! So how can I make it simple?"

"Let's go back to your years as a teacher to see if we can find our answer. The plaque and note from your students said you were remarkable. Why did you get into teaching?"

"That's easy! I love kids. They were my family. And I felt like I was making a difference."

"Anything else?"

"I cared. I remembered what it was like when I was their age, when I was in their shoes. I recall being frightened and nervous at times, needing someone to talk to or to hold my hand and help me feel like everything would be okay."

"And what was your ultimate goal for these kids?"

"That they would grow into responsible adults. That they would care about what they were doing. That they too could— and would—make a difference."

"So where did money fit into the equation?"

"It didn't."

"So you *simply* focused on making a difference, instead of making a dollar while teaching?" Rolly concluded. "Your priority was *simply* the outcome, rather than the income."

"I really, *really* like how you put that! When my kids knew I was passionate about them, they became passionate about what I was teaching."

"If you think about it, Sherri, your kids bought *you* because you put them first—because you cared about them—and *then* they bought what you were teaching."

"You're right, Rolly. That's exactly what happened."

"Then why not try that in *this* career—in your 'real estate classroom,'" he suggested. "What would happen if you were to put *these* 'kids' first? If they knew you cared about *them*? If they knew *they* were more important than the subject you were teaching—in other words, the product you were selling?"

"I think my results would be very different."

"I agree. You see, the most important thing you have to offer, Sherri—the most important thing you're selling—is YOU. It's who YOU are. It's what YOU represent. You do that by caring, by being there when they need someone to talk to. You do that by holding their hand when they're frightened or worried, by helping them feel everything's going to be okay.

You see, it's YOU! That's what YOU offer. YOU are the most important thing they will ever buy!"

"I'm sad to admit that's not what I was selling, not even close. I wasn't selling caring. I wasn't selling being there. I wasn't putting myself in their shoes or being someone they could really talk to. I wasn't making it about them. Now that I think about it, I wasn't being me! No wonder I struggled these past months. I just got right down to business with them, knowing this business offered more financial opportunity. Is wanting to make money a bad thing, Rolly?"

"There's absolutely nothing wrong with wanting to make money. In fact, it's a good indicator of the value we're adding to the lives of those we serve. The more money we're making, the more value we're adding. But should money be our purpose, Sherri? *That's* the question we should be asking ourselves."

"I don't think money should *ever* be our purpose!"

"I agree. Many get into sales from professions where they didn't necessarily make a lot of money, but they had a higher purpose. It might have been making the world a safer place, caring for others, or doing behind-the-scenes work to bolster the success of others."

"I know lots of people like that, people who are emotionally fulfilled," Sherri said.

"When they—just like you—can retain their higher purpose, sales offers an opportunity to enjoy both emotional fulfillment *and* financial fulfillment," Rolly insisted.

"I see that clearly now. That seems so simple to me."

SIMPLE . . . for Me

That *is* the first part of SIMPLE," Rolly explained. "Take your notepad, and beside 'SIMPLE,' write 'for me' to the upper right."

$$\underline{S}IMPLE \cdots for\ me$$

"This will remind me to stay true to my purpose—to keep it 'simple . . . for me,'" Sherri noted. "So what's the second part of SIMPLE?"

"To answer that, we're going on an Easter hunt."

"You mean an Easter *egg* hunt?"

"No, an *Easter* hunt. Do you have anything scheduled in the morning?"

"I'm free as a bird."

"I like that," Rolly chuckled. "I need to say goodbye, so why don't you plan on meeting me at nine. I'll text you the address later."

Sherri looked puzzled. "You already have my number?"

Rolly hopped to the floor and proceeded toward the door. "I've had your number a while. A little bird told me!"

"That's cute, Rolly, and I can't wait to learn who that little bird is," she said, following him. "Do I need to bring anything with me tomorrow?"

"Your pen and notepad, your winning personality, and your lovely smile."

"You're sweet! May I open the door for you?"

"Only if when I say 'thank you'—which you know I will—you don't say 'no problem'—which you know you will."

"That is what I would say. Is that wrong?"

"Think about it, Sherri. 'No problem' sounds like you were just doing a job, or a chore, that might have been a bother, an inconvenience, or a problem. Whereas . . ."

"Oh, I understand where you're going," Sherri said. "Whereas 'you're welcome' or 'my pleasure' or 'it's my privilege' or even 'I'd be honored to' shows respect and manners—that I *wanted* to. I promise never to say 'no problem' again. Please allow me to get the door."

Rolly strutted through the open doorway with a smile. "Thank you, my dear lady. How considerate of you!"

"It's my pleasure," she replied. "And I'm looking forward to tomorrow!"

"Me too!" Rolly shouted as he flapped his powerful wings and took flight. "Have a terrific evening!"

Sherri watched her newfound friend disappear into the sunset. She placed her phone and the notepad and pen on the coffee table and found herself anticipating tomorrow's meeting with Rolly. Sitting on the loveseat again, she realized how different she felt. The frustration and anxiety that overwhelmed her earlier were replaced by a sense of peace and tranquility. For the first time in this new career, she felt hope. And of all things, that hope had arrived on the wings of a bird.

Rolly's visit had already taught her several lessons. He had made their time together enjoyable. More important, he had made her laugh.

"Maybe I need to have more fun with my clients," she

thought. "I tend to be serious, too businesslike. I need to make buying and listing homes enjoyable for my clients—and for me."

Then Rolly's impeccable manners came to mind. He was so polite, so courteous, so thoughtful. And best of all, it was genuine. He wasn't trying to gain her good favor. She could tell he meant it, that it came from the heart. Maybe that's one of the reasons she trusted him in such a short time. "It's clear I need to use better manners," she sighed. "I guess my parents were right all along."

Glancing at her phone, Sherri remembered Rolly's lesson in phone etiquette. "I also need to have better phone manners when I'm *with* people," she muttered to herself. "I answer calls and check text messages and emails when I'm with clients, other agents, and my broker. I do the same with Charlene. Come to think of it, I do it with *all* my friends. And I do that with Carly and John David. I even do that to Doug. No wonder they often feel disconnected from me. I've got a lot of things I need to change. And if I'm going to hold myself acCOUNTable, I need to write these things down so I can be reminded."

Accountability List—Day 1

Picking up her notepad and pen, Sherri flipped to a new page and began making a list. At the top she wrote

Sherri's Accountability List—Day 1

Then she jotted down points that immediately came to mind:

☐ *Have more fun.*

☐ *Use manners.*

☐ *Set phone to "Respectful" while with others.*

"As important as these are," she thought, "learning about Mary Kay Ash's sign was perhaps more important. Rolly made me feel so important when he showed interest in my family, my plaque, my home, and my teaching career. I need to focus on making the other person feel important, because they are."

☐ *Notice things.*

☐ *Make the other person feel important.*

The notion of putting people first and product second came to mind. "If I truly believe in making others feel important, then I must put people first. Putting people first will make a monumental difference with my clients."

☐ *Put people first and product second.*

She thought of all her listing appointments. "I'll bet if I put these things ahead of trying to get the listing, I'd not only get more listings, but I'd get them at a realistic price because people would trust me and be open to my advice."

Just then, her eyes caught the subtle movement of something under the edge of the chair. Looking closer, she saw it was Rolly's feather. The ceiling fan must have blown it off the coffee table. She picked it up, recalling how soft his feathers were when he gently hugged her.

"I don't hug enough either," she thought. "I would hug my kids at school every day. They loved it. I'll bet my grown-up kids in my 'new classroom' will too. That's going on my list for all those who are open to a hug."

☐ *Offer hugs.*

Reviewing her list, she felt proud that she was doing the two things Rolly had requested. First, she was demonstrating a desire to learn. And second, she was holding herself acCOUNTable. "This is not going to be a problem," she declared and quickly added two more items to her list:

☐ *Hold myself acCOUNTable.*
☐ *Replace "no problem" with "my pleasure."*

She paused, savoring how energized she felt and how happy. "I need to reflect this happiness and my positive outlook. I will strive to wear a smile every day and make others around me smile and feel happy."

☐ *Always wear a smile.*

"And knowing that I'm the most important sale I'll ever make should really make me smile. That's an absolute must!"

☐ *The most important sale I will make is me!*

Scanning the list to see what she'd overlooked, Sherri found herself replaying the discussion about her time in the classroom.

She had shared with Rolly how making a difference in her students' lives had been fulfilling and motivating. And inspiring her students to also make a difference had been a worthwhile purpose. "I *simply* focused on making a difference instead of making a dollar," she said aloud, echoing Rolly's summation. Then with a keen sense of purpose, Sherri added one more item.

☐ *Focusing on my purpose will help keep it* <u>S</u>IMPLE . . . *for me!*

"I can't wait to tell Doug about this when he gets home. He is going to be so"—and then it hit her. "I can't tell Doug about any of this. He'll think I've lost it! A visit from a talking parrot who came to teach me how to **S.M.I.L.E.**"

She'd have to give some thought as to how and when she would describe the events of this pivotal day.

SIMPLE . . . for My Guests

Arriving a good twenty minutes early at the address Rolly had texted, Sherri parked across the street and surveyed the grounds where her Easter hunt would take place. It was a beautiful property, well maintained, and on a quiet street with mature oak trees that shaded the entire front yard. "Someone takes a lot of pride in this place," she thought. "I can't wait to meet whoever lives here."

As if on cue, Sherri received a text from Rolly instructing her to come through the side gate and around to the back yard when she arrived. Switching her phone to the "Respectful" mode, she placed it in her handbag along with her notepad and pen. And with a bounce in her step, she headed that way.

She found Rolly perched on the handle of a gardening cart and sporting the brightest smile. "Good morning, Sherri. I had a feeling you might arrive ahead of time. Being respectful of other people's time is very important."

Greeting him with an even bigger smile, she extended her arms to share a hug. "You're welcome, Rolly. I may be a lot of things, but late isn't one of them!"

"I love the 'you're welcome' I just heard as opposed to 'no problem.' You're a fast learner."

Sherri held up her hands with enthusiasm. "Just holding myself acCOUNTable. I've got some new habits to develop if I'm going to learn how to really **S.M.I.L.E.**"

At that moment, a distinguished-looking gentleman appeared from a lush vegetable garden. He quickly put aside the bucket of tomatoes he had just gathered and hurried over to his guests.

Rolly spoke up. "Sherri Montgomery, I'm proud to introduce you to Bob Easter. He has offered to teach you the second part of SIMPLE."

As Bob shook Sherri's hand, he also placed his left hand over hers and patted it gently. "Sherri, it is an absolute pleasure to meet you, and I love your smile. Rolly has told me so much about you. I feel like I've known you for years."

"You're *the* Bob Easter? Of Easter & Easter, Realtors?" she asked. Then she winked at Rolly, signaling that she understood the Easter "hunt." "I love your company, Mr. Easter. By the way, I also love this gorgeous property!"

"Thank you so much. We are blessed to live here. And please call me Bob." Sherri nodded, accepting this request.

"I founded my company when I was much younger and was passionate about growing people," Bob explained. "Now organic gardening is my passion, along with fruit trees."

Bob picked up the bucket and began walking toward the back patio. "If I might suggest, let's ease over to the shade of the pergola where we can enjoy some of the—if you'll pardon the pun—'fruits' of my labor."

"I would be happy to. It looks so inviting," Sherri replied and extended her forearm to give Rolly a lift. "May I do the honors again, sir?"

"Why yes, you may, my dear," Rolly responded, puffing up his chest.

Bob set the bucket of tomatoes on a countertop. From the outdoor fridge, he removed a bowl of freshly sliced peaches and placed it on the patio table, along with plates and utensils.

"Sherri, why don't you sit here facing the garden." Addressing Rolly, he added, "Since you'll be leaving shortly, why don't you have Sherri drop you at your regular placemat over there."

Sherri positioned Rolly so he could step to his spot. "You won't be staying, Rolly?"

"I'm being introduced to the owner of a swimming pool company in hopes that I can help them grow. But I wanted to be here to give the two of you a proper introduction. You'll be well cared for with Bob. I've nicknamed him the 'Master of SIMPLE.'"

"'Simple-minded' is what my wife calls me," Bob joked. "But Carolyn loves me anyway."

"Too cute. Will I get to meet Carolyn today?"

"I hope so," Bob replied, returning from the fridge. "She's on a conference call but should finish in a bit." He placed a tray on the table with pitchers of milk, orange juice, and ice water. "I know Rolly always prefers water. Would you care for the same, Sherri, or would you prefer orange juice or a glass of fresh milk? Or . . . I could make you a Bloody Mary from my prize tomatoes. What's your pleasure?"

"Such tempting offers. Well, a Bloody Mary is what I want, but the orange juice is what I need. So orange juice, please. And thank you, Bob, you're a delightful host."

"He is that—and more!" Rolly asserted as Bob poured her juice. "So, Bob, why don't you share the second part of SIMPLE with Sherri."

Before Bob could respond, Sherri spoke up. "Rolly, I don't mean to interrupt, and I am very excited about learning the second part of SIMPLE, but if it's okay, I'd first like to learn a little more about our host." Turning to Bob, she eagerly spilled her list. "I'm interested in hearing how you got into real estate. And what you did before that. Where you were born and raised. How you developed a passion for gardening. And I would love to hear more about Carolyn and your family. Please, tell me a little about yourself."

"I would be happy to, Sherri," Bob consented, "as long as I have the opportunity to learn the same about you."

Rolly was finally able to get a word in. "It's obvious the two of you see the sign each is wearing, so I'll give you both all the time you need all to yourselves."

Rolly opened his wings to give Bob a hug. "As always, my friend, I thank you for your willingness to give back to others. You'll be pleased to know you have a great student here who will take to heart what you have to share." Then he exchanged a hug with Sherri. "Take good notes and ask lots of questions. What Bob is about to teach you is a dramatic departure from what you've likely learned or have ever seen done in real estate. It's big!"

"I will!" she replied. "And good luck on your meeting. Oh, before I forget, when will I hear from you?"

As he took flight, he yelled, "Bob will set that up!"

Sherri and Bob began enjoying the fresh fruit and drinks, settling into the personal discussion they requested. A good thirty minutes of laughter and conversation passed before they moved on to the subject at hand.

"Bob, your story is amazing! From delivering newspapers as a young boy to becoming the director of circulation for a major newspaper, your determination and work ethic are an inspiration. And then you decide to start your own real estate firm. I'm impressed."

"Thank you. Both careers have been fulfilling. As for you, I admire the self-confidence you have to give up a secure income in a profession where you've excelled to take a chance on a brand-new commission-only career. That takes courage."

"It's been a little scary. But now I see hope. I've learned more in the past sixteen hours than I've learned in the past sixteen weeks. I'm excited and honored to be mentored by you!"

"Well, I'm delighted to help you," Bob replied. "Let's see if we can add a little more to what you've learned."

Sherri opened her notepad and turned to the page with the "SIMPLE . . . for me" reminder. "So please tell me about the second part of SIMPLE."

"First, it's important we don't confuse the idea of simple

with easy. There can be times when simple requires a lot of time and work. In fact, we'll likely spend more time on the second part of the *S* in **S.M.I.L.E.** than on any of the remaining letters combined."

"I appreciate your being up front, but that doesn't deter me. I used to tell my students that a person cannot succeed without hard work. I'd pull out the dictionary and remind them that it's the only place where 'success' comes before 'work.'"

"I love that. And as you know, putting forth time and effort doesn't just apply to schoolwork or careers. It's the same for relationships." Then he smiled, pointing toward the bucket of tomatoes. "It even applies to gardening."

"That's true," Sherri agreed. "So I will devote my time and effort to my new career. I just want it to appear effort*less* . . . and natural."

"With practice, it will. So let's begin. Who else would we want to make things simple for besides you?"

"For my clients?"

"Yes, but let's broaden that to 'for my *guests*.'"

$$\underline{S}IMPLE \quad \substack{\ldots\, for\ me \\ \ldots\, for\ my\ guests}$$

"I noticed Rolly using 'guest' instead of 'client' or 'customer.' I'm curious what the distinction is. Aren't those just words?"

From Words . . . to Character

I respectfully suggest that the words we use make *all* the difference," Bob said. "Do you have your cell phone with you?"

Taking out her phone, she said, "I do, but I switched it to 'Respectful' so I could give you my full attention."

Pulling his out of his pocket, Bob revealed he had done the same thing. He raised his phone to touch hers, as if making a toast. "I believe it was Goethe, the German writer and statesman, who said, 'Things which matter most must never be at the mercy of things which matter least.' Though Goethe was born more than two hundred years ago, it's as if he was warning us about these things."

"I often feel at the mercy of my cell phone. But this morning I had coffee with an old friend and applied what Rolly taught me about phone manners. We had the most relaxing time together, just visiting and focusing on each other."

"Being present while *in* the presence of others is one of the greatest gifts we can give someone."

"Wow, Bob! Goethe doesn't have anything on you. I've got to write that down. May I quote you?"

"I'd be honored, Sherri." He paused briefly and then continued. "Now on your phone, please Google the word 'customer.' What is the definition?"

"It says 'a person or organization that buys goods or services from a store or business.'"

"Does the term 'customer' describe the people you're doing business with?"

"I guess it would for the *one* customer who did purchase from me."

"You mean for the *family* who purchased," Bob said, politely rephrasing.

"They *did* buy, but it's obvious you would prefer I call them 'family' instead of 'customer.' Again, not to sound disrespectful, but do the words I use really matter?"

"It doesn't if your focus is on making a dollar. But Rolly told me you wanted to make a difference, that you were more concerned with the outcome than the income, as you were when teaching. If that's true, then the thoughts you're thinking conflict with the words you're saying. You're thinking *people* thoughts but using *business* words. And those business words will cause you to act more businesslike, in a less personal manner. Practicing closes, overcoming objections, all those steps of your training. Remember those?"

"Do I ever! And I didn't like the results or the way I felt using them. So how do I change that?"

"You seem to be doing well with signs," Bob pointed out. "You certainly saw me wearing one today when you made me feel so important."

"Thank you, Bob. For me, visualizing signs is a powerful reminder. Now everyone I see is wearing a sign. I saw my husband, Doug, wearing one last night, so I asked him about the concert with his friends. We ended up talking for hours and not just about music but about everything. I could tell he was surprised I was so interested." She giggled. "I was tempted to tell him something 'flew' over me, but I didn't."

"That's funny!" Bob agreed. "And a great story about Doug. So have you noticed the different signs hanging on the posts of the pergola we're sitting under?"

"I did. And I wanted to comment on them. But I decided to devote my full attention to our conversation."

"I appreciate your being present. So now take a moment to read the sign directly behind you."

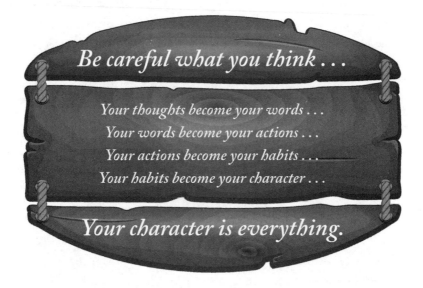

Be careful what you think . . .

Your thoughts become your words . . .
Your words become your actions . . .
Your actions become your habits . . .
Your habits become your character . . .

Your character is everything.

"That's powerful!" she remarked. "It clearly shows how your thoughts, your words, your actions, your habits, and your character are all linked—one influences another."

"And when all is said and done, it *is* all about character. It's the qualities, the values, the principles that we admire in the people we trust. In the business world, character plays a critical role in choosing those with whom we do business." Bob leaned in toward Sherri. "And character becomes crucial in helping you, Sherri, because I—along with the other business leaders you will meet—will be sharing techniques that will enable you to influence others."

"I hadn't thought of that," she responded.

"If these techniques are used to take advantage of others—*out* of character, if you will—to get others to do what they may not want to do or don't see a value in doing . . ."

"You mean to purchase something so I can make a sale or to earn a commission?"

"Yes," he replied. "If used for the wrong reasons, the other person will see right through them. In essence, all the techniques intended to help us will only hurt us."

"I believe that wholeheartedly. If I have the slightest inkling I'm being 'sold' something, I'll turn right around and walk out. So instead of thinking of my clients as customers, which is a *business* relationship, I should think of them as guests, a *personal* relationship."

"Precisely," Bob confirmed.

"So to clarify, 'guests' refers to people who have not yet purchased, and 'family' refers to those who have."

"Correct. Now, let's look at a deeper meaning of these terms. What comes to mind when you hear the term 'guest'?"

" 'Guest' evokes a feeling of hospitality, the way we treat those whom we invite to our home. We thank them for coming, and we make them feel important and comfortable, as you did with me."

"Because I was selling you something?"

"No way, Bob. You did it because you care."

"I do care. So, do you understand what the second term 'family' implies, should you decide to embrace the ideas and techniques I'm offering?"

Sherri thought about her own family for a moment. "To me, 'family' signifies closeness, trust, loyalty. We are honest with family. They can depend on us. We'll always do what's right with family and never take advantage of them. So I guess when we turn guests into family, we'll treat them the same way—which is how we'd all love to be treated."

"That sums it up beautifully. So are you buying?"

"I am!" Sherri declared. "Just call me family!"

Sherri visualized how she could recast herself in this new role yet sensed there was still a lot to learn. "I presume there is more to making it 'SIMPLE . . . for my guests' than just how I refer to them."

Jars of Jam

Very perceptive, Sherri. We've barely begun to scratch the surface. Let's focus on where you're spending most of your time—on listings or sales?"

"On sales. I mostly handle the phones."

"When you get a call, what do you typically do?"

"I try to get their name, the property they're calling on, and a little about what they're looking for. Then I meet the people at the property to tour it."

"Then what?"

"Since no one has ever bought the first property I've shown, I think of properties I know that are similar in size, location, and price and suggest looking at those, too. Unfortunately, with the same outcome—no sale. Then I return to the office and search the MLS for everything that matches their criteria and set up a tour of these properties as soon as their schedule permits."

"How many might that be, and over how many days?"

"Obviously, it depends on a lot of things. But it can be anywhere from twenty to thirty, sometimes forty to fifty properties. And that can take two to three or more days."

"And this has happened with how many guests?"

"Over the past three months, sixteen . . . eighteen . . . somewhere around there. But only one has purchased. It is frustrating and exhausting. These people are wearing me out!"

"Have you considered how *they* might be feeling?"

"You think they feel the same way?"

"Wouldn't you?" Bob reasoned.

"I guess that's possible. They certainly don't seem to be having fun. So what's the solution?"

"You ever thought of making it simpler, for everyone?"

"You think I'm making it too complicated?"

"To answer this, let's look at the research of Dr. Sheena Iyengar, a professor at Columbia Business School. She has earned an esteemed reputation in the psychology of choice. I heard her give a TED Talk that described an interesting study involving—of all things—jars of jam."

"I love jam so I am all ears!" Sherri exclaimed.

Bob smiled. "Dr. Iyengar set up a tasting booth with a variety of gourmet jams at an upscale grocery store. Sometimes it had six flavors, and sometimes it had twenty-four. The goal was to see if the number of choices affected the number of jars of jam sold. So what would conventional marketing wisdom tell us?"

After some critical thinking, Sherri made her prediction. "The more choices shoppers have, the more likely they are to purchase since additional options will help them find one they consider the best—one that perfectly fits their taste." She paused, applying the situation to real estate. "So I think jam is like properties—the more choices a person has, the better!"

"That may *seem* logical; however, Dr. Iyengar's findings showed the *opposite*. Though a higher percentage of shoppers stopped to sample jam when offered twenty-four varieties, only three percent made a purchase. But of the shoppers who stopped when offered only *six* varieties of jam, thirty percent made a purchase. So what conclusion can we draw?"

"Having too many options makes choosing more difficult?"

"Exactly," Bob agreed.

"Did the findings surprise you?"

"Not at all. My real estate team and I had already learned to show only five to seven properties to most of our guests. Five to seven, that's all."

"Really? And did you notice that your number of choices was in line with Dr. Iyengar's six jars of jam?"

"I did. But what's even more amazing is that well over thirty percent of our guests purchased one of our jams . . . I mean, our properties. That's what was *most* exciting!"

"I'm impressed! But how do I get my guests to be okay with viewing only five to seven properties?"

"The answer is questions . . . and a change of scenery."

"I assume you're going to explain both."

"After I compliment you on how quickly you have begun changing your thoughts and words. Guest sounds so much better coming from you, Sherri. Now let's look at the actions that will become your habits. Do you ever Skype?"

"On occasion, Bob. Why do you ask?"

"Because you're going to meet a lady who was unable to

join us here today. But through the marvels of technology, she will help explain 'change of scenery.' Since it's getting a little warm out here, I suggest our own change of scenery. Let's go inside to the kitchen table. It will take me just a few minutes to connect her on my laptop."

"Sounds great," Sherri said cheerfully. "Since I'm now family, I'll refresh our drinks. Would you like me to put the pitchers of milk and orange juice in the kitchen fridge?"

"That would be greatly appreciated. And I'll bring the bucket of tomatoes."

A Change of Scenery

When Sherri joined Bob at the kitchen table, she saw a woman's image on the laptop screen. "Sarah Thomas, please meet Sherri Montgomery," Bob said, making the introduction.

After Sherri and Sarah exchanged pleasantries, Bob continued, "Sarah is the managing broker for PSW Real Estate. They specialize in urban development in the downtown area. She was their first and only sales person for several years, and as the team grew, she moved into sales management. Sarah is currently on a sabbatical, of sorts, raising two toddlers, which is why she couldn't join us here today. To date, she has been one of Rolly's brightest success stories. Sarah, I'll let you take the floor now."

"Thank you for the kind introduction, Bob. Prior to joining PSW, I enjoyed a successful career as a real estate agent in Chicago. Based on that success and my experience, I was recruited to sell their properties here. Because of the prime location of their two communities and the level of amenities, these properties came at a much higher cost per square foot than average—a figure that told me I was really going to have to sell to make this work. Can you see and hear me okay?"

"Doing fine," Sherri replied. "I love war stories from someone who has been in the trenches."

"You're about to learn this soldier earned her stripes the hard way. So thinking I needed to create as much value as I could in the offerings—and as quickly as possible—I would meet a guest and immediately emphasize our standard features: granite countertops; top-of-the-line, name-brand appliances; the insulation package and green building standards, just to name a few. I featured, functioned, and benefited everything! If we had it, I talked about it. I closed, I trial closed, and I overcame objections. The only thing that would have made my tie-downs any better would have been to use an actual rope!"

"And your results?" Bob asked.

"My results," Sarah responded, shaking her head. "I'll give you results. Of the nineteen properties at these communities, I sold only five in my first nine months, despite getting good traffic and having a high level of interest on the part of my guests. And I'm ashamed to say it, but I had to significantly discount the few I did sell."

"Those are better numbers than I've had," Sherri revealed. "I've sold only one property in three months."

"Thanks for trying to make me feel better," Sarah sighed. "But with all due respect, selling an average of one home every two months was not a stellar performance for someone with my experience. And keep in mind, Sherri, these were new homes in prime locations."

"Bob mentioned you were one of Rolly's brightest success stories," Sherri noted. "Can you tell me what changed?"

"Everything changed when I met Rolly. He helped me recognize the value of putting people first and product second. He also taught me to visualize the sign people were wearing and to focus on creating a memorable experience. I even changed the words I used. Customers became guests and many became family. He reminded me to use good manners and make the experience fun. I learned so much in a short time."

"I can relate to everything you've covered thus far."

"The most significant thing Rolly taught me was the simplest of all. He suggested I change the scenery," Sarah stated.

"I was hoping you would get to that." Sherri leaned closer to the screen. "I'm taking notes. Please continue."

"Our situation was a little unique in that I didn't have a furnished model like most builders or a dedicated sales office. Most people would call off our signage or contact us via the Internet, and I fielded all those calls and emails."

"I'm in a similar situation, handling the calls and Internet leads too."

"That's good to know. So Rolly asked how I would typically handle those calls or requests. I explained that I'd do my best to answer questions such as pricing, size, and availability and then encourage them to meet me as soon as possible, which most would. Then I'd go into my dog-and-pony show, trying to wow them with what we had and how much I knew. The results were disappointing."

"So what did Rolly tell you to do?"

"He didn't *tell* me to do anything. It's what he *asked* me that helped change the way I looked at things. His questions offered a new perspective."

Sherri recalled how Rolly had her invert the curved lines to see the difference in changing her perspective. "So what questions did Rolly ask?"

"He began by wanting to know what I learned about the people I was meeting. Where did they live now, and had that always been home? What attracted them to downtown and this lifestyle? What did they do for a living? What did they do for fun? Were they active? Did they enjoy walks in the park? Canoeing? Jogging? Hiking? Biking? How did they spend their free time? Had they enjoyed any of the cool restaurants and local hangouts for which this area was famous?"

"And did you know the answers to these questions?"

"About my guests? No, I was too busy selling my tail off. Did I know what attracted most people to this area? Yes, but not because I asked them. I lived downtown and enjoyed these amenities myself. As for the change of scenery, Rolly began by asking if I embraced the people-over-product idea. I told him I totally did, that I'd much rather learn about people than talk about product. Then he asked another question that felt like it came out of left field. He wanted to know if my parents ever took me to a candy store when I was little."

"That would get my attention!"

"When I told Rolly that I loved trips to the candy store, he asked yet another question. He wanted to know what my focus was the entire time I was in that store. Well, that was easy. Candy, of course! Candy was *all* I would talk about, *all* I could see, *all* I could think about! Then it dawned on me. I was inviting my guests to meet me at my candy store. And I'll bet you can guess what we talked about while there."

"So thinking about the candy store taught you a lesson about sales," Sherri noted.

"A big lesson! When I met guests at the property, we talked only about the property—my product, my candy. I didn't make them feel important. We didn't connect. I knew nothing about them."

"So what did you do?"

"I decided to change the scenery. Instead of meeting at the property, I suggested we meet for coffee or for breakfast, for happy hour, for whatever. And I would suggest we meet at one of the area's popular hangouts—a coffee shop, a restaurant, or a gelato bar. In other words, we'd meet at a *cooler* candy store."

"And I can guess what you discussed over food and drinks," Sherri teased.

"You're right, food and drinks," Sarah replied. "That's the candy at these businesses. But as we enjoyed fabulous items on the menu, I also took the time to get to know my guests. I asked about their professional pursuits, their backgrounds, their favorite pastimes. I would also try to discover something about my guests that they had in common with others who were there, the owners, the chef, the servers, even the patrons. And since I was a regular patron and had formed relationships with these people, I simply introduced my guests to them and shared their commonalities. Then they would begin a lively conversation while I watched the magic happen."

"I can picture that and it's brilliant! But can I assume not everyone would agree to meet you off-site?"

"The vast majority welcomed my suggestion. They loved it! For the few who preferred meeting at the property, I would take the time to get to know them over food and drinks there. If there was a refrigerator at the property, I made sure it was fully stocked with an array of refreshments and beverages. If it didn't have a fridge, I'd pack a picnic basket and cooler and bring refreshments to the property."

"So whether at a favorite hangout or on-site, when did you start talking about your product?" Sherri inquired.

"When *they* brought it up! I waited for them to turn their sign around—the other side of Mary Kay Ash's sign that read, **'*Now* you can tell me what's important that I need to know!'**"

"How observant," Sherri remarked. "I never thought of there being two sides to the sign. So, what happened after this change of scenery?"

"There was a remarkable change. Over the next four months, thirteen guests became family members."

"That's incredible!" exclaimed Sherri, jotting the numbers down to compare the before and after. "That's almost six times what you had been selling!"

"That's right. Moreover, the new sales were all full price!" Sarah added. "And the increase in sales, along with higher profit margins, helped PSW expand into four new markets in three states."

"What a story!" Sherri enthused.

"I enjoyed sharing it," Sarah said, glancing over her shoulder. "But if you will excuse me, I hear someone stirring. Feel free to call, Sherri, with any questions. Just understand if I don't answer, I'm either up to my neck in diapers or I have my cell on Respectful mode and I'll return your call. Goodbye, Sherri. Goodbye, Bob. I hope I was able to help."

"More than you know," Sherri said.

"Bless you for all you do!" Bob added.

Decisions

Bob, it's amazing how that one simple adjustment made such a difference. So did you apply this change of scenery idea too?"

"Yes, I did. Like Sarah, I recognized the challenges in meeting guests at a listing. But the thought never occurred to me to meet them at a neutral site like a coffee shop or restaurant. What I did instead was encourage my guests to come to my office."

"And they would actually do that?"

"When I explained it was to better serve them and to save a great deal of time and frustration, the majority would. They understood my sincerity and the benefit to them."

"What about those who wouldn't meet at your office?"

"I'd make a business decision. I would consider how much business I had going on at the time—properties to preview, tours to schedule, properties to show, closings to book, agreements to wrap up. Then I would decide whether I had time to do it their way, knowing it would require more of my time and likely produce fewer results."

"So you might not meet with those guests?"

"It would depend. If I could do it the preferred way, I could likely find the right property for them in no more than two days. If I did it their way, it could take three to four, even five, days of my time. So if my appointment calendar was full, I would refer them to one of my newer agents who might have more free time. Does that make sense?"

"Perfect sense," Sherri said. "There's only so much time available each day. I would rather spend four days helping two guests find a home than four days helping just one guest. That's a smarter way of doing business."

Sherri allowed herself a few moments to ponder this philosophy. "So tell me, Bob, about the things you did and said with those guests who would come to your office."

"I'd begin with SIMPLE . . . and a smile. I wanted to treat them as I would treat a guest in my home. I'd serve refreshments. I'd offer to hang up their coat or jacket. I'd ask if the room temperature was okay. I'd let them know where the restrooms were. I'd suggest a comfortable place to sit. I tried to make them feel at home. And I'd see the sign hanging from their neck and make them feel important."

"And when did you get to the topic of real estate?"

"When *they* brought it up. The more time I spent learning about my guests as people, the less time I needed to spend learning about their situation and showing product. Forming a strong relationship with my guests helped build trust. Trust is the most important thing in any relationship."

"I seem to recall those exact words from Rolly. So after building trust, describe how you got down to business."

"The change of scenery provided a change of focus away from product and toward people," Bob said. "Then the business discussion focused on questions to reduce the jars of jam. Allow me to borrow your notepad, so I can show you how to set this up. First, I'd turn the notepad in a landscape position and divide it into four areas, labeling each like so."

Have Now . . . ?		
Like . . . ?	Dislike . . . ?	Change . . . ?

"Why turn it sideways?"

"It reminded me to be *different*. I cannot overemphasize the importance of that simple act. You see, Sherri, everyone else is focused on what the guests are *looking for*, the *solution* they're hoping to find, the *dream* they're in search of. But there's a much more productive place to start. I focused on what they HAVE NOW. I'd ask them to describe where they currently live in great detail while I took thorough notes. I'd want to know the style, size, layout, number of stories, room count, age, condition, maintenance expenses, and utility costs. I might even suggest they draw the floorplan. I wanted to see their world through their eyes. I even asked for pictures if they had them."

"That is a different approach."

"I'm just getting warmed up, Sherri. If the home was on a homesite or acreage, I wanted to know the size, topography, trees, views, drainage, well or city water, septic or city sewer, above- or below-ground utilities, easements, outbuildings, and any improvements they'd made."

"At some point did you also address location, traffic congestion, neighborhood, neighbors, noise, safety, schools, convenience to shopping, current zoning, tax rate, and property values? And I assume if you ran out of room to record their answers, you'd continue on a second page."

"Very perceptive!" Bob said, commending Sherri. "My goal was to learn everything they'd be willing to share, and then some. It's the 'and then some' where it really gets good. I began addressing it with three questions, the first of which is a feel-good question. I asked, 'What do you LIKE about what you have now?'"

"I'm guessing you asked this because whatever they like about what they have now, they would likely want to have, if possible, in what they're looking for. I must ask why you refer to it as a feel-good question?"

"Their answer allows them to feel good about their current home and about their decision to live there. This line of questioning starts on a positive note."

"That makes sense."

"Next, I asked what they DISLIKE about what they have now, hoping to learn about the discomfort, the problems, the pain they associate with that property. And it's that pain that has them contacting me. The pain, Sherri, gets us to the 'why,' instead of the 'what.' See the difference?"

"It's night and day," Sherri responded. "I read that most people are more likely to be motivated by escaping pain than acquiring pleasure."

"It was Tony Robbins who made that statement. He was explaining what compels people to take action—we want to rid ourselves of what hurts."

"So if you initially focus on what hurts—what causes the pain—and then progress to what they are looking for— the pleasure—you will get answers that are more accurate and relevant."

"Exactly!"

"Then if the second column gets to the why, what's the purpose in the third? Wouldn't the answers to what they want to CHANGE be the same as the things they disliked?"

"It often is the same. However, I've learned that it can be a challenge to get some people to talk about the things they DISLIKE about where they live now. Some can get so attached to what they have now they almost feel like they're attacking a friend. It can feel very personal."

"I can see that."

"Also, some may feel describing what they DISLIKE implies they made a mistake in choosing where they live. And it's difficult to admit to a bad decision, a mistake. That's why I also ask if there's anything they'd like to CHANGE. This sounds less critical and can be easier to answer."

"I can relate to that. I don't *dislike* anything about my husband; however, there are a few things I might like to *change*. And marrying Doug was certainly not a mistake!"

"Well said! So do you see how people might be more responsive to the CHANGE question?"

"I do," Sherri stated. "But I don't see why you need to ask about what they HAVE NOW four different ways? And why do you write their answers down?"

"Let's start with the four boxes. The more we learn about their taste in 'jams,' describing the jam they have in their pantry now—what they like, dislike, and what they would change about that flavor if they could—the fewer jars of jam in our tasting booth. We'll know more about what they're LOOKING FOR."

"That is smart!" Sherri exclaimed.

"It's actually more akin to *wisdom* than *knowledge*," Bob replied. "To understand the distinction, think about my home-grown tomatoes. Knowledge would be knowing that a tomato is actually a *fruit*."

"I didn't know that. So what is wisdom?"

"Wisdom is knowing *not* to put them in a *fruit salad*."

Sherri chuckled. "Knowledge versus wisdom . . . there is a huge difference!"

"I would say so. Let's discuss three more boxes that will also prove to be important. For this, I'd flip to a clean page and draw this set of boxes and labels:

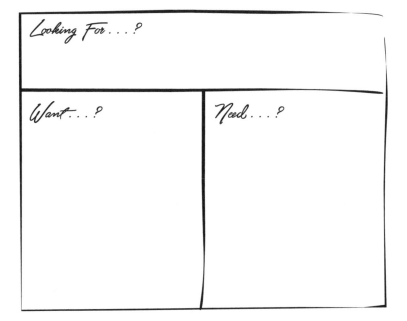

"The discussion of what they're LOOKING FOR is usually straightforward, and their answers help me envision what that looks like. To get more specific, I then ask what they WANT and what they NEED in this new property."

"That sounds helpful, Bob. But what's the distinction between WANT and NEED? They seem the same to me."

"Do you recall when I offered you a selection of drinks earlier?"

"You gave me choices of water, orange juice, milk, coffee, and—who could forget—a Bloody Mary with your home-grown tomatoes!"

"Good memory, Sherri. And do you remember your response?"

She smiled. "I said the Bloody Mary was what I *wanted*. but the orange juice was what I *needed*."

"See the difference?"

"Clearly. A WANT would be on a wish list. It would be nice to have but might not be practical. But a NEED is more of a necessity, perhaps even a requirement."

"You got it. A built-in outdoor grill with a rotisserie might be a WANT whereas a portable grill will suffice."

"But a handicap accessible home for a family member who uses a wheelchair would be a NEED!"

"Yes. Separating their answers into these two different categories allows you and your guests to have a realistic discussion about what would be *nice* versus what is *necessary*. That's very important as it also helps further reduce the number of jars of jam!"

Save Time . . . Reduce Stress

After all these questions, what if you do end up with more than five to seven properties that match what they're searching for? What if you find twenty or thirty?"

"That would be unlikely," Bob said. "But if it did happen, I would preview all the properties first—by myself. I'd explain that unlike most agents who show ten to fifteen properties per day, my goal is to show only half that number in total to save them time and minimize their stress."

"They would appreciate that!" Sherri said, remembering her own exhaustion.

"I don't want my guests to feel rushed when walking through what could be their home. I want to allow an hour or more to view each property as opposed to the ten to fifteen minutes agents usually schedule."

"That's about all I was spending," Sherri revealed. "And when you factor in driving time between properties, you can't spend more time if you're trying to tour ten or fifteen in a day."

"You're right. But seeing fewer properties in a day gives your guests more time to get a truer sense of what does and doesn't work in each home."

"So what would they do during that hour, Bob?"

"We would consider the functionality of the rooms. If they entertain, we could discuss food preparation and set up, traffic flow, plus what they envision doing with their guests in the different areas. I might have them imagine arranging their furniture, selecting their children's bedrooms, or celebrating Thanksgiving dinner with their family."

"I see the power in that. And the more time they spend in a home and can see themselves *living* in it, the more attached they can *become* to it."

"Precisely! So let's go back to my reason for previewing the homes beforehand. In a day, I can typically visit the twenty to thirty properties by myself. Then taking what I know from the two lists we have created, I can comfortably select the top five to seven properties to view with them the following day."

"Okay, but does that really save time? You will spend two days doing it your way—one to preview the properties and one to show them, when I can show them the twenty to thirty properties in the same two days."

"Is your desire to *show* or to *sell* properties?"

"Ouch! Good point, Bob."

"It's back to the jars of jam, Sherri. Too many choices resulted in fewer jars of jam being purchased. It's the same with too many properties. People are overwhelmed when they have too many options and they can't make a clear choice. So five to seven keeps it stress free . . . and simple."

"And my goal is to keep the process SIMPLE . . . for me . . . and my guests."

"It has to be," Bob agreed.

"One last question. What about videos and virtual tours? Would you consider viewing these with your guests to narrow down the choices?"

"That may sound tempting, but I go back to Dr. Iyengar's experiment with the jars of jam. Do you think viewing twenty-four videos about jam would help people select one they want to purchase?"

"Probably not," Sherri admitted.

"I would agree. But some guests may still insist on viewing the videos. So just keep in mind the result may be more time and more stress, neither of which is good."

Rules of Shopping 2-4

N ow let's move on to your second question," Bob continued. "You wondered why it's important to write down your guests' answers. Has Rolly told you about his **4th Rule of Shopping?**"

Sherri quickly thumbed through her notes. "I don't recall his mentioning that. And I assume there are at least three other rules I also need to learn."

"There are actually seven—three of which I will address now. You might want to write these down. We'll begin with the **2nd Rule of Shopping:**

We prefer to buy from people we trust.

"I couldn't agree more. Trust is essential in doing business with someone. If I don't trust a sales person, I'll go out of my way to shop elsewhere, even if it costs more."

"Most people feel that way too, thus the rule. So what makes you trust someone, Sherri?"

"I trust people who are genuine and truly care about me, who try to understand where I'm coming from, people who take the time to listen."

"Interestingly enough, the **3rd Rule of Shopping** pertains to listening. It says

We can be influenced by someone who listens.

"So true. But most sales people seem to think the opposite, that you influence people by talking. Much of what I learned about overcoming objections was how to use prepared responses to persuade the other person to accept or believe *my* answer."

"Did you learn about the value of asking questions to better understand where your guests are coming from?"

"That wasn't emphasized. And I would get especially frustrated when my guests would end up arguing with me."

"Then you'll likely appreciate Rolly's **4th Rule**:

We don't argue with our own answers.

"What a coincidence! That's the same philosophy I had with my kids in the classroom. If I gave them the answers, they seemed to question them. But if I led them to the answers, they believed them. They owned them."

"Now do you understand the importance of writing their answers down?"

"Absolutely! You record *their* answers so they won't argue with them later. It *is* that simple," Sherri reasoned. "So let me see if I understand the process. Once I've determined what they're LOOKING FOR, I can enter that into my MLS search. And the possible list of properties to consider could range from five or six to fifty or sixty."

"It could," Bob said. "And since the recommended number to show them is five to seven, you're where you need to be if your search identifies five or six. That's just enough jars of jam to likely find one they'll want to buy."

"But if it's fifty or sixty"—Sherri looked over the boxes Bob had drawn—"I can use their answers to what they LIKE and DISLIKE and what they'd CHANGE about what they HAVE NOW to reduce the list to a smaller number of properties, fewer jars of jam. And if I'm not quite to the five to seven range, I can refer to their answers about what they NEED and what they WANT to narrow their choices even more."

"You're almost there. Now tie all of this back to having their answers written down."

"Okay, the reason I should write their answers down is so they won't argue about needing to see everything that pulled up in my initial search. I can refer to their answers as to why those properties don't work, and they aren't likely to argue with them."

"Now you've got it! That's the difference between knowledge and wisdom. Knowledge is the awareness of what's

available in the marketplace that initially fits what your guests
are LOOKING FOR. And that knowledge is good."

"But if you want to go from good to *great*, you need wisdom. And wisdom is having their answers to your questions
to help them see that only a few select properties, which *they*
selected, truly match what works for them."

"Very good. What your guests are LOOKING FOR gets
you to the 'what.' Whereas the HAVE NOW questions get you
to the 'why.' A big difference!"

"*All* the difference! You've really made simple—SIMPLE
for me and SIMPLE for my guests. I thank you!"

"And I thank *you*. I'll give you a few minutes alone to
gather your thoughts and make some notes. We have covered
so much today."

Accountability List—Day 2

Wow!" Sherri said to herself. "Today is going to change
everything for me and for my guests. Not only what I do
but *why* I do it. Where do I begin?"

She flipped to the new page she'd prepared.

Sherri's Accountability List—Day 2

As she reflected on the day, Bob's patio sign and his comment about character came to mind. "In the business world,
character plays a monumental role in choosing those with
whom we do business."

She came to a decision. "I must pay a visit to the family
whose listing is overpriced. I took that listing to benefit myself,

knowing there was little to no chance it would sell that far above market price. That wasn't fair to them. So to be true to my character, I must help them see the value in lowering the price or cancel the listing. Regardless of the situation, my character should steer my path."

☐ *Let character be my guide.*

"Character is the reason you switch your cell phone to Respectful," she recalled. "And if I'm truly respectful to my guests, I will listen attentively, and they will feel understood, acknowledged, and safe. Being present with others builds trust."

☐ *Being present is the greatest gift you can give.*

Thinking of other ways she could better serve her guests, Sherri recalled Dr. Iyengar's jam study. The findings were eye-opening. "While I thought I was *helping* my guests by offering numerous choices, I was actually *hindering* their ability to make a decision."

☐ *Limit the number of "jams."*

She recognized the first step to paring down the choices would be asking the four questions from the first list. When followed by the questions from the second list, the remaining choices would likely be a more reasonable number. "These steps need to become part of what I do with all my guests. This will save time and eliminate a world of stress."

☐ *Learn what they LIKE, DISLIKE, and would like to CHANGE about what they HAVE NOW.*

☐ *Discover what they're LOOKING FOR, along with what they WANT and what they NEED.*

"And Rolly's three Rules of Shopping . . . how big are those! I can't wait to learn the other rules," she thought. "Writing their answers down so they can't argue with them later will be paramount and proactive. Like the two aspirins and water that Rolly's brother set out each night, that will take care of problems before they *become* problems!"

☐ *Write their answers down!*

Then the frank discussion they had about time and business was so impactful. Applying the lessons she learned would undoubtedly be a timesaver.

☐ *Make a business decision based on my time.*

"And Sarah was so helpful and had such an inspiring story! If I put people first and create a memorable and enjoyable experience for my guests, I'm bound to make a significant difference. I'll never go in a candy store without thinking of Bob and Sarah. How simple is that one adjustment!"

☐ *Change the scenery. Find a better "candy store."*

As Sherri finished her list, Bob returned to the kitchen. This time he was not alone. "Sherri, I'm proud to introduce you to my better half. This is my wife, Carolyn. Sweetheart, this is Sherri Montgomery, our newest superstar."

As Sherri instinctively extended her hand, something told her a more appropriate greeting was due. "Carolyn, would you accept a hug instead? Bob has made me feel . . . well, like family."

Carolyn graciously accepted the offer. "We are family, and Bob has told me so much about you. He has very high expectations. Based on what you're learning from Rolly, Bob, and Sarah, you're going to do great!"

"Thank you for the encouraging words. I'm anxious to put all this into practice. I know I'll need to be patient, as it will likely take some time before I see results."

"I beg to differ, Sherri. You'll begin seeing results immediately!" Bob predicted. "In fact, Rolly wants you to take the next few days to apply what you've learned so you can start experiencing that success. He wants you to call him Thursday at 5:00 p.m. and is hoping your schedule is open Friday evening. Just check his text message for his phone number. Now to close our morning together, please allow us to walk you to your car."

"Oh, I'm fine. You don't need to bother."

"We never let family leave without being escorted to their vehicle," Bob replied. "It's our pleasure."

Sherri felt the thoughtfulness of that simple gesture. And their warm goodbye even included to-go cups of juice and water!

"What a sweet couple!" Sherri thought as she drove away.

"And Bob has to be one of the most genuine and kindhearted people I've ever met. No wonder he has been so successful. I'd buy anything from him!"

On FIRE!!!

Hello, Rolly, this is Sherri. I know I'm calling a little early, but I couldn't wait to speak to you. Is it okay?"

"You bet it is, Sherri. How have you been?"

"I'm on FIRE!!!" she cried. "I'm having so much fun; you're not going to believe what happened!"

"Why don't you try me."

With that invitation, Sherri began recounting the events of the past few days. And her exhilaration was palpable. She explained that after reviewing her notes, she recognized an opportunity to start over with several guests she had worked with over the past few months. So she reconnected with a couple who was still in the market to buy and invited them to breakfast at a quaint restaurant on the water near where they had been looking.

After greeting her guests with a warm smile and a hug and switching her phone to Respectful, they chose to do the same. "Eliminating that distraction seemed to change the dynamics of our visit," she told Rolly.

For the first forty-five minutes, Sherri devoted her attention to getting to know her guests and was amazed at how much she learned in such a short time. She mentioned to Rolly that she kept seeing the signs they both were wearing.

When Sherri discovered that the wife's family owned a restaurant, she introduced her guests to the owners of the restaurant where they were eating, and they hit it off. Like Sarah, she watched the magic happen as they shared their backgrounds and favorite recipes. The couples exchanged phone numbers and even made plans to go to a sporting event together the following week.

Sherri added that when the couple eventually asked how the real estate market was doing, she took that as her cue to get down to business. Pulling out her notepad and pen, she began focusing on what they HAVE NOW, what they LIKE and DISLIKE, and what they would CHANGE. With each answer, she gleaned a clearer picture of the situation they were hoping to escape.

When the questioning shifted to what they were LOOK-ING FOR, including their WANTS and NEEDS, it all came together, for everyone. Their answers led to five properties, so she scheduled appointments for the next day. "And I still can't believe it!" she exclaimed. "They fell in love with one home, and their offer was accepted that evening!"

"Congratulations! I'm so happy for you. So what did you learn from this experience?"

"I learned that what you and Bob and Sarah taught me works. And that was with using just the *S* in **S.M.I.L.E.** I think the *S* should stand for all of you being so smart."

"Hardly. It worked because you believed in *yourself.* You trusted what we shared and applied it. And at any point were you thinking about the commission you might earn?"

"Money never crossed my mind. Instead, I kept envision-ing Bob's sign about character. It impressed me so much I can-celed my listing that was overpriced. I couldn't get the owners to price it within reason, so I felt I was doing them a disservice, and that wasn't fair to them."

"I applaud you for that!"

"Thank you. So back to my story. I simply focused on helping my guests. They were like excited kids as they toured the properties and imagined themselves living in each home. It was so gratifying, but I'm still surprised it happened so quickly."

"Your story reminds me of Trevor Wilson's," Rolly mentioned.

"Who is Trevor? Am I going to meet him next?"

"Not unless you're headed to Florida. Trevor is a young man who recently learned how to **S.M.I.L.E.** He sells RV resort property for Carefree Communities in the Tampa area and had toured sixty-three people over the previous eight months with no success. He realized he'd been putting product first and paying little attention to people."

"I'll bet he was frustrated and wearing a frown."

"Not anymore. In the two weeks after learning to **S.M.I.L.E.**, he saw nine guests, and three of them became family members. He was on fire too!"

"Good for him and good for his families! So why didn't you share his success with me earlier?"

"You might have argued with *my* answer."

"You're right, but I can't argue now—your **4th Rule of Shopping**! So what *really* happened, Rolly? I understand that I changed the scenery, made it fun, made them feel important, and built trust. But I wonder what made them buy so *quickly*. Was I just lucky?"

"That depends on what you mean by 'luck.' Darrell Royal,

the famed football coach from the University of Texas, would inspire his players with the pithy saying 'Luck is what happens when preparation meets opportunity.'"

"With that definition, I would be considered lucky. But I still feel I'm missing something. Can you give me a hint?"

"Think about the expression 'When the student is ready, the teacher will appear.'"

Sherri was puzzled. The expression was familiar, but she had always approached teaching from the opposite perspective. She felt a teacher had to understand the reality of her students before her lesson could be meaningful to them. "When the teacher is ready . . . the student . . . will appear," she thought. With those words, the poignant message on her plaque came to mind. " 'Education is not the filling of a pail, but the lighting of a fire!'" she exclaimed. "Is that what you're saying, Rolly?"

"Substitute one word and you'll understand why your guests bought so quickly."

" 'Selling is not the filling of a pail, but the lighting of a fire!' That's it! When my guests shared what they DISLIKED and would CHANGE about what they HAVE NOW, they recognized their pain—the pain they wanted to get away from. That lit a fire under them!"

"Now do you understand why talking about your product without first diagnosing the pain seldom works? It's what Sarah struggled with. It's what Trevor struggled with. They had been trying to fill a pail instead."

"I had been too! If I didn't know better, I'd think Doug's dealership might know about the *S* in **S.M.I.L.E.** His sales team had the best week they've had all year."

"Who knows, Sherri, perhaps they got lucky too."

"Could be, Rolly. Oh, I meant to ask you, did you get lucky with the swimming pool company?"

"I did, and thanks for asking. The owner, Keith Zars, is the nicest man. He's excited that his team will soon be learning how to **S.M.I.L.E.** So I believe you're ready for the next letter. I'll send you a text later with the address of where to meet tomorrow at 4:30 p.m. See you then!"

Section 4:
The *M* in S.M.I.L.E.

To Relationships—the ME Paradigm

The GPS directed Sherri to a small café quietly situated in the corner of a shopping center. While parking, she noticed a sharply dressed man exiting the side door to a patio area and carrying Rolly on his forearm. After locking her car, she quickly headed that way.

Perched on a barstool, Rolly extended his wings to give Sherri a hug. "So thrilled you could join us. And thanks for making the long drive."

"I'd have driven across the country just to see you."

Rolly spoke up to get the attention of the man Sherri had noticed. "James Smothers, I'd like you to meet Sherri Montgomery. Sherri, this is James."

James politely shook Sherri's hand, being careful not to drop the serving tray he had just tucked under his left arm. "Sherri, it's an honor to meet you. And please forgive me. I was searching for a serving tray when you arrived. We asked to sit out here for privacy, but the outside bar isn't open yet. So I'm going to get our drinks. What could I get for you?"

"It's a pleasure to meet you, James. And how very thoughtful of you. I'll have a sweet tea. Would you like some help?"

"No, ma'am. You're our guest," he said. "It's my pleasure." With tray in hand, James hurried back inside.

"James is one of the most considerate people you'll ever meet," Rolly stated. "He is all about serving others."

"I sensed that!" Sherri said with a grin.

"Before we begin, I wanted to hear how your dinner went with Charlene?"

"How nice of you to ask. Doug and I had a wonderful time." Sherri shared the details about the special evening and their friendship with Charlene. "Her relationship means the world to both of us."

James returned with the drinks. Having overheard Sherri's final comment, he proposed a toast, "Here's to relationships, both old and new."

"To relationships!" they repeated in unison.

"James is here to help you learn about the *M* in **S.M.I.L.E.**," Rolly explained. "He has mastered this letter better than anyone. Like Sarah, he was one of my best students."

"You have a knack for surrounding yourself with extraordinary people," she noted.

"I wish I could take credit, but it's not my doing," Rolly replied. "Like you, James was referred to me, which may have a little bit to do with why we're here."

"Or maybe a lot," James added with a smile.

"James came to me as a top producer with thirteen years of new home sales and sales management experience. He was at the top of his game."

"Congratulations, James," Sherri said.

"Thank you. But I just did what I was trained to do. I take no credit for what I accomplished."

"I respect your humility, but I imagine hard work on your part played a role."

"My parents had a good work ethic, so I was definitely raised to work *hard*. But thanks to Rolly, I learned the value in working *smart*," he said. "In my former work paradigm, it was my job to *sell* the home and my builder's job to *build* it. But Rolly introduced me to John Norris by way of video. That made a huge impression on me. John helped me understand that smart sales people do more than sell. They *also* build. They build *relationships*. And it's up to *me* to make that happen."

"I take it the *M* in **S.M.I.L.E.** stands for ME?"

ME

"Yes, it's up to ME to build the relationships. That's the first part—and the first part of John's story. Since Rolly knew John personally, I'll ask him to do the honors."

"John Norris came to new home sales having enjoyed a thirty-year career in retail, where the stores under his direction flourished," Rolly recounted. "Why? Because he trained his staff to build strong relationships with their guests. Feeling so valued, those guests, in turn, brought their friends and family to shop there, too. And the process kept on going. John created a vibrant shopping experience and credited their success to referrals."

"What struck me was John wasn't in the retail business," James interjected. "He was in the people business. For him, it was all about people and the relationships he and his team built."

"Can you share specifics about what he did?" Sherri asked.

"He started with many of the things you and I discussed when we first met, including what you learned from Bob and Sarah," Rolly revealed. "John's team focused on making everyone feel important. They learned about the guests who shopped at their stores, where they lived, where they grew up, what they did for fun and work. They learned about family, both immediate and extended. They'd make note of and remember names, including pets!"

"And they'd only talk about an item in the store when a guest brought it up?" Sherri speculated.

"You got it," Rolly said. "And John's team sent thank-you notes to guests for visiting. They'd call to let them know about new items coming to the stores. They'd send mailers with coupons or invitations to sales events. And with each visit, they would continue to build, to strengthen the relationship. So when John changed his career path to new home sales, he focused his energy and talents on what he knew best—building relationships."

"I imagine that worked out well," Sherri said.

"He took a struggling neighborhood that had averaged fifteen sales per year and turned it into the company's top-selling neighborhood, averaging 125 sales annually. And ninety percent of those were referrals from the relationships John had built."

"Was there anything else John did? I ask because I know people who are good at relationships but don't get that many referrals."

"That's the second part of the story James will share."

The WE Paradigm

J ohn also introduced me to an entirely different paradigm, one that turned ME into WE. And this turned my world upside down."

"That sounds intriguing. Please continue!"

"Well, I presume Rolly discussed the importance of seeing things from a different perspective."

She flashed a big smile at Rolly. "Vividly! Showing me how curved lines could turn into a smile produced an image I'll never forget. Now I view everything through that image of a smile."

"We're about to do something similar. Across from the word 'ME,' write the word again, except this time turn the *M* upside down. What do you have now?"

Sherri flipped the letter. "The word 'WE.'"

"And that, Sherri, is what John helped me see. Not a conventional business paradigm built around ME, but an unconventional, upside-down model for growing my business built on the philosophy of WE."

"I hope you're going to explain this new model."

"He's going to do better than that, Sherri," Rolly spoke up. "He's going to take you to a live demonstration of the power of WE. You ready for a little drive?"

"You bet! Where are we going?"

"You two will enjoy dinner at the home of a family who purchased from James. I am headed home to have a milestone dinner with my bride. Gwen and I are celebrating our twentieth anniversary today."

"Rolly, I knew you had siblings and that one was married. But you hadn't mentioned Gwen. How exciting! James, did you know this was Rolly's anniversary?"

"I did. John taught me to learn about and make note of special occasions whenever possible with everyone I meet. I know birthdays and anniversaries. I know dates of upcoming weddings, birth announcements, graduations, and special religious ceremonies. I even know pets' names and birthdays, and I send cards for all of these. As John suggested, I also send thank-you notes to everyone."

"I never thought birthdays and special occasions and thank-you notes were important in business," Sherri said.

"When our business is people and we build relationships, it's everything."

"I see that now. So, Rolly, I know your brother's secret to a happy marriage. And now that I know you're married, may I ask what yours and Gwen's is?"

"When we got married, we decided I would make all the big decisions and Gwen would make all the little ones. And for twenty years, every decision was deemed a little one!"

Sherri burst out laughing. "You continue to remind me how important it is to have fun. Will you *promise* to enjoy your evening with Gwen?"

"Only if *you* promise to enjoy yours with James. Call me tomorrow at 5:00 p.m., and you can tell me all about it."

She wiggled her fingers. "You can *count* on it!"

After exchanging hugs, Rolly took flight.

"We'll keep John's legacy alive!" James hollered as he and Sherri waved.

Changing Clubs

Thank you for offering to drive, James. So where are we going?"

"To see Randy and Marge Kiolbassa. They purchased a home from me two years ago. They, like the other families to whom I had sold homes over the years, were members of my 'Love 'Em and Leave 'Em' club."

"I'm not sure I'd want to join that club."

"You wouldn't! I called it that because I would love them while they were buying and then leave them after they closed. While under contract, I'd check in with them every few days, update them on the progress of their home, and monitor the status of their loan. But after they moved in, I would move on to the next sale. It wasn't intentional. I just didn't know any better."

"Did you franchise that club?" Sherri joked. "The agent who sold Doug and me our home did the same thing. Keeping in touch while we were in escrow, but after we closed, not another word! I notice you said the Kiolbassas *were* members. So have you formed a different club now?"

"I have. All my families are now proud members of my 'Ambassadors' club, and I treat them the same before, during, *and* after they close, just as John did. I use the term 'ambassador' because my families have become my personal envoys. They promote *who I am* and *what I do* to everyone."

"So they send you referrals?"

"Better than that! They *bring* me referrals. Once you see the WE paradigm in action, you'll understand the secret to getting the most out of it."

The Quality Introduction

Arriving at the Kiolbassas' a few minutes early, James parked across the street. "The secret to the WE paradigm is what John called a 'Quality Introduction,'" he told Sherri. "My Ambassador families will set up a personal, face-to-face introduction of the friends or family they are referring to me."

"And they will actually bring them to you?"

"Yes. Or better yet, they'll invite me to join them at their home, which is why we're here this evening. You're about to witness the power of a Quality Introduction. Let me grab this gift for our hosts, and we'll head inside."

"Please come in, James," Randy said, accepting the gift and giving him a bear hug. "What a pleasure to see you, my friend. And you must be Sherri. I'm Randy and so glad you could join us. Are you okay with a hug too?"

"I am, Randy," Sherri replied. "Thank you for having me. And you must be Marge," she added, greeting the lady standing beside him. "It's wonderful to meet you."

"I'm delighted, Sherri. Welcome to our home," Marge said, offering a hug. "And, James, it's always a pleasure. Thank you for coming."

"I always cherish my time with the two of you," James declared as he and Marge embraced.

"Dinner will be ready in about fifteen minutes, so please join us in the living room," Marge requested. "We have some friends we'd like you to meet. Jim and Paula Clark, please meet James Smothers and Sherri . . . Montgomery? James texted your name earlier. Did I get it right?"

"You did, Marge," Sherri said warmly. "Jim and Paula, it's a pleasure to meet both of you."

"It absolutely is," James agreed. "So how long have you two known Randy and Marge?"

"We met them six months ago at our church," Jim replied, "and felt a rapport with them from the start."

"Jim and Paula recently moved here from out of state," Marge explained. "They're leasing a home nearby and had intended to stay there for a while. But they came over for dinner Monday night and fell in love with our neighborhood."

"They fell in love with our home, too," Randy added with a grin. "But we told them it's the last one of this design in the neighborhood. So we took them to see the home you're framing on the next block."

"We really weren't in the market to buy yet," Paula said. "But after Marge and Randy told us about you and how terrific you've been and how fun you've made the experience—plus the quality of the homes you build here—we thought we'd better meet you before you're sold out."

"Is that home still available?" Jim asked. "Because if it is, we'd like to see it again in the morning."

"First, I want to thank you for the kind words," James said. "As for the home under construction, I believe it's still on the market. Our model just closed, and I haven't heard of any agreements submitted today. I'll confirm that this evening and set up a time to see it tomorrow. Before we make those arrangements, I want to thank Marge and Randy for getting us together. They have introduced me to six families—no, you would be the seventh—of which four, I'm proud to say, are now homeowners here."

"Marge and Randy have already given us a lot of valuable information," Jim remarked. "They've told us about the included amenities and the added options, which we're thrilled about. Plus, the price is where we need it to be."

"If we are able to select a few of the interior colors, we could be your fifth family," Paula shared. "Randy and Marge are your best advertisement for this neighborhood!"

"Not to mention the best sales people," James added, winking at them. "They are the king and queen of my Ambassadors. Of course, you two are welcome to dethrone them. I have several second-generation Ambassadors who are close to doing just that."

"Hey, we're up to the challenge," Paula replied. "We are the first of several families relocating here. My company will be transferring others in the near future. So we'll be sure to get you in touch with them before they arrive."

"I would be honored," James said graciously. "And before we sit down to enjoy the delicious meal Marge and Randy have prepared, I brought a bottle of champagne to replace the one you keep chilled for special occasions such as this. Was I wise in doing so?"

"Chilled and ready to uncork!" Randy offered.

"And we have just enough time for a toast before dinner is served," Marge added. "Can everyone join us in the kitchen to celebrate?"

Sherri helped Marge get the champagne glasses from the cabinet as James uncorked the bottle and filled each one. With glasses raised, Randy offered a toast. "Here's to our newest neighbors, to our dearest friend and best sales person ever— though we have never thought of him as a sales person—and to our newest friend who joined us tonight. To relationships, that's what it's all about."

"To relationships!" everyone chanted.

Sherri was stunned. Not by the toast, though it was identical to the one an hour earlier. It was the experience. She'd never seen or expected anything like this. Friends . . . helping friends . . . helping friends. All because of the deep relationship James had built with this family.

The meal was divine, as Randy and Marge proved to be excellent cooks. But what Sherri enjoyed most were the conversations that took place over dinner. James wanted to learn everything he could about Jim and Paula. "He obviously saw the signs they were wearing," she said to herself.

She noticed how James related so much of what he learned about them to what he knew about Randy and Marge. He connected the two families in ways they had yet to discover about each other. James also made a point to include her in the conversation, asking about her family and her teaching background.

Knowing these referrals were providing a significant boost to his income, Sherri paid attention to how he and the events of the evening were perceived by both families. No one seemed to feel that James was motivated by money. In fact, his commission seemed to be the farthest thing from his mind. He was laughing and having fun, and so were they. He was smiling and hugging, and so were they. He was loving what he was doing, and so were they.

Following dessert and more stimulating conversation, James

and Sherri gave their goodbyes and expressed sincere thanks to everyone for a wonderful evening. As hugs were shared, James shared that the home on the next block was still available and confirmed meeting with the Clarks the next morning.

While driving back to the restaurant, James sensed Sherri's awe regarding the evening. "WE is a powerful concept, isn't it?"

"That's an understatement! I'm at a loss for words!"

"I felt the same after my first Quality Introduction. You're welcome to use this time to reflect on this experience as I drive us to your car. And please know you're safe. I only had a tiny sip of champagne."

"Me too since I have a long drive. But what a great way to celebrate such a special occasion," she said. "And thank you for the time. I think I will use it to add to my notes."

Accountability List—Day 3

She turned to a page where she had entered

Sherri's Accountability List—Day 3

The first thing she made note of was the importance of relationships. "If I want to really **S.M.I.L.E.**, then building relationships must make my list. And I should combine that with what I learned about the ME paradigm—that it's up to ME to build them and to work smart."

☐ *If I want to S.M.I.LE., it's up to ME. Smart sales people build relationships.*

"The success John Norris enjoyed both in retail and home-building was amazing," she reflected. "But the beauty of how he did it was in its simplicity. His referral business thrived because he was in the people business."

☐ *I will build my business on referrals by getting into the people business!*

Then her thoughts turned to what happens when you turn ME into WE. "That unconventional, upside-down paradigm of growing my business built on the philosophy of WE is where the real opportunities lie. The WE gets ME the referrals. I'll make a special notation to help illustrate that."

☐ *It's up to ME to turn . . .*

"This note will definitely help me remember!" she thought. And since remembering special occasions was a meaningful way to help build relationships, she added that to her list.

☐ *Remembering special occasions helps build relationships.*

That led to thinking about James's two clubs; seeing the Ambassador club at work during dinner really hit home. "I don't want to be known as someone who forgets about my families after they buy. I will hold myself acCOUNTable to staying in touch."

☐ *Staying in touch helps maintain the relationships.*

As she added that to her list, James pulled up to Sherri's car. "Perfect timing!" Sherri said. "James, if you have a few extra minutes, I do have a couple of questions about the Quality Introduction."

"I'll gladly make time, Sherri."

"Thanks. Let's find a quiet table inside. This time, I'm buying."

Secrets of a Quality Introduction

They found a secluded booth in the corner of the main dining area. "James, in my training I was taught to simply ask for referrals." Reaching in her purse, Sherri pulled out a business card to show him. "In fact, this is what they suggest we put on the back."

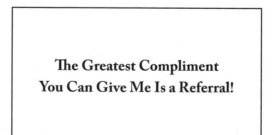

**The Greatest Compliment
You Can Give Me Is a Referral!**

"Would it be just as effective to hand this to someone?" she asked.

"I don't think John would have said it's a bad idea. But the question he would likely ask us is whether it works as well as a Quality Introduction."

"I don't think it can hold a candle to what I just witnessed."

"I agree. Did you happen to notice the floor plans and information from my neighborhood on the coffee table where Jim and Paula were sitting?"

"Yes, and I was curious where those came from. Did you give those to them when I wasn't looking?"

"Directly, no. Indirectly, yes. I had given those to Randy and Marge weeks ago. John shared that he would give something larger than a business card for his Ambassadors to give to families, something that served as a bigger reminder to share their experience with others. Business cards are too *commonplace* and too easy to *mis*place."

"That's smart!" Sherri exclaimed.

"It is! Another smart thing John did was to ask his Ambassadors this question: 'If you've enjoyed this experience, would you tell your friends and family about it, whether they're looking for a home or not?' Whereas most people ask, 'Do you know of someone who might be looking for a home?' And why is that important? Because we all know plenty of people we'd be willing to tell about a great experience. However, the odds of us knowing someone who is in the market for a home at any given moment are slim at best. You see the difference?"

"Clearly. And Paula mentioned she and Jim weren't really in the market to buy a home."

"You were paying attention!" James noted. "And when his

Ambassadors did come across someone, John requested they give him a Quality Introduction. So they would bring those guests to meet him in person—whether at his office or in their home—and he would promise to treat his new guests the same way he had treated them."

"John's service was personal—and professional!"

"Definitely! And there are three other reasons why the Quality Introduction is so powerful. Let me write these down for you."

1. The referred guests will show up.

"I can see that, James. They won't stand up the family who's referring them. They'll be there."

2. It saves time.

"I would agree. Just look at the work Randy and Marge have already done for you. All you have to do tomorrow is tour the home with Jim and Paula and find out if they can choose some interior colors. If they're satisfied, you can simply write up the agreement."

"You may experience something similar with the Quality Introductions you receive when people are shopping for a home," James added. "Your Ambassadors may have already sold them on the neighborhood, the schools, and the location. Perhaps they've even driven them around, pointing out homes that are for sale."

"I'd be okay with that," Sherri smiled. "So what's the third reason?"

3. *The best sales people are present.*

"My Ambassadors are real, Sherri! They're believable. If they tell a family they need to live here or this is the best time to buy or they need to stop looking around, the referred family is far more likely to believe them. If I were to say those things, they could easily question my motives."

"That's understandable, James, since you're in sales. If I recall the numbers correctly, the Clarks will become your fifth referral sale from the king and queen of your Ambassadors club. Plus you're getting strong support from the others. Is it making a significant difference?"

"Good question. Let's look at a then-versus-now comparison. The thirteen years I ran the Love 'Em and Leave 'Em club, I had less than five percent of my sales from referrals. Through my Ambassadors club with Quality Introductions, I just exceeded the sixty percent milestone. I'm not quite to John's ninety percent, but I've definitely taken my game to a whole new level. Best of all, I'm getting more help each day."

"I assume the ME into WE paradigm has been financially rewarding."

"Let's just say my company, my sales manager, my banker, and my wife are all very happy."

"Don't take this the wrong way, James, but I see my potential for success going beyond yours. Working for a builder, you can help only guests who want to buy in *your* neighborhood. Whereas I can help guests purchase homes in *any* neighborhood. Combine that with the fact that I can also get referrals from my guests who are listing their homes, and the potential is even greater."

Self-Originated Opportunities

Believe it or not, Sherri, it's far greater than that. John's WE also included self-originated sales that came from local businesses, places of worship, and even schools. In a three-year period, John received ten referrals from a local dry cleaner, eight from a pie shop, five from a delicatessen, and another five from the local schools, just to name a few."

"Wow! So why were they all so willing to help him?"

"Because he first helped them. He referred them business from the families who bought from him. And those same families who helped the local businesses grow helped fill the schools with their children and the places of worship as new members. He tried to help everybody he knew."

"It's just people helping people!" Sherri exclaimed. "The ultimate WE. And I can do the same with the Ambassadors club I'll create. I'll start with my one homeowner, plus the other guests in my pipeline. Then I'll quickly shift my focus to those self-originated sources, beginning with Doug's dealership. I can send them the people I know, and they, in turn, can send their people my way. My contacts in education will be next, along with all my friends, plus all the places where I do business."

"Excellent plan! So did we get to all your questions?"

John's Legacy

I do have an informal question I've been wanting to ask. As Rolly was leaving, you assured him we would keep John's legacy alive. Is John no longer with us?"

Looking away briefly, James took a deep breath before continuing. "Very perceptive, Sherri. In body, no. In spirit, yes. He's alive through others. We saw it in Randy and Marge. It will continue with Jim and Paula. You and I and others who know his story will keep his legacy alive. WE have to!"

Sherri clearly sensed John was so much more than a successful sales person. "I'm . . . so sorry. Was his health failing when he changed careers?"

"No, John's wife of thirty-four years was diagnosed with stage four breast cancer. Distraught, he switched careers to be home in the evenings with her. She survived three years. Sadly, John passed away two years later, after losing a hard-fought battle with ALS—Lou Gehrig's disease. Sherri, I hate to end our conversation on such a serious note."

Sherri managed to regain her smile. "I think John would want us to celebrate. Thanks to you and John, I'm leaving here inspired. I know it's up to ME if I want to **S.M.I.L.E.** And I'll proudly turn ME into WE. I'm leaving committed to getting into the people business and building my network of relationships and referrals."

James walked Sherri safely to her car. "You're right," he decided. "We have so much to celebrate!"

The Little Stuff *Is* the Big Stuff

Good afternoon. This is your five o'clock wake-up call. The weather today will be partly cloudy with a high of eighty-two degrees," Sherri stated, grinning from ear to ear.

"How cute!" Rolly chuckled. "Do you actually think that's why I'm having you call at the same time each day?"

"I was curious. I thought you might not know that the early bird gets the worm."

"I'm actually more into fruits and nuts. And I don't have to get up at dawn to enjoy them."

"I hear you. And speaking of enjoyment—and food—how was your anniversary dinner with Gwen?"

"Very memorable! Thank you for asking. We enjoyed a romantic candlelit dinner while listening to the Eagles and danced on the patio to 'Peaceful Easy Feeling.' Just the two of us in the desert with a million stars all around."

"And did you give her sparkling earrings as a gift?"

"You know your Eagles' songs!"

"They're my favorite group. Doug and I saw them in concert several years ago. It was an unbelievable show!"

"To *show* you what a small world it is, Sherri, you actually have something in common with Don Henley."

"*The* Don Henley. Are you serious?"

"As serious as I can be. Just as you were referred to me, a dear friend named Christophe referred a mortgage banker to me. His name is Joe Brown. While in college, he played in a band called Felicity with . . . Mr. Don Henley."

"It *is* a small world. And how did you learn that?"

"Over lunch the day Joe and I met. When you're in the *people* business, you'd be surprised what you can learn when you invite people to tell their story. And yes, I gave Gwen earrings, and they looked absolutely stunning on her."

"How sweet, Rolly. If you don't mind, I have two questions for you. The first may sound a little foolish: do birds have ears?"

"That's not foolish at all. In fact, it's an appropriate question since you can't see ours! Yes, we do have ears. They're hidden under feathers that protect the ear openings and reduce the wind noise. Gwen just clipped the earrings to her feathers, and we danced the night away. So what's your second question?"

"It involves Joe Brown. Knowing you, I'm anticipating he too has learned how to S.M.I.L.E. If so, could I ask you for a Quality Introduction? I'd love to help him by referring my families his way. At the same time, I know I'd also be helping them through the higher level of financial services I'm certain he'd provide."

"You don't miss anything, do you? Yes, I've had the privilege of helping Joe and his entire team. I will gladly make that introduction as soon as he and his wife, B. J., return from a business trip. Speaking of business, at some point, I would also like to introduce you to a lady in the title business to whom I was referred. Her name is Camille White. She and her team also know how to S.M.I.L.E. and would provide an extraordinary level of title services for the families you could refer to her."

Sherri realized she and Rolly could talk the afternoon away. "'That would be wonderful and a big help! But, please forgive me for taking up your time with all this little stuff. I know this doesn't have anything to do with why you wanted me to call."

"It might not have been the purpose of having you call, but when you're in the people business, there's no such thing as little stuff. Everything you and your guest choose to talk about should be viewed as big stuff."

"I guess that ties back to Mary Kay's sign. 'Important' can cover all kinds of stuff!"

"Yes, it can. You gave me a fun 'wake-up' call, then asked about our anniversary dinner, which led to our discussion about the Eagles and Don Henley—and Gwen's earrings. Then you wanted to know if birds had ears! All of that made me feel important. And I thank you. You're doing great at holding yourself acCOUNTable!"

"Thank you, Rolly, but I wasn't consciously trying to do that. I was just being myself."

"Being yourself is as important as anything I can teach you. Remember YOU are the most important sale you'll ever make. Never feel like you should be in a rush to get down to business. Your guest will tell you when it's time."

"That's exactly what Bob and Sarah told me."

"And they're right. Until then, savor those special moments with others. That's how relationships are built."

Growing My Business

I'm glad you mentioned relationships. My time with James totally changed my paradigm of how I want to grow my business. I'm already working on building the relationships for my own Ambassadors club."

"That's wonderful. James tells John's story so well. In fact, it's better than told—it's lived!"

"I started living it on my drive home last night. I reached out to the Carters, the couple who purchased from me because they felt sorry for me."

"You say that, but I've got a strong suspicion it was more because they trusted and believed in you. Good people like to help good people become successful."

"Whatever the reason, I was able to meet them for breakfast this morning and learned about their neighbor who wants to sell her home. They were so gracious and called her to set up a Quality Introduction tonight at their home. Isn't that amazing?"

"Sounds like luck to me!"

"Yep!" Sherri said, sensing his playful sarcasm. "Preparation and opportunity will make anyone lucky. But here's something you might find hard to believe. As we were leaving, I noticed they were driving a new car from Texstar Ford Lincoln. Now that's not unusual; Doug's team sells lots of vehicles. But here's where it gets interesting. I dropped by their service department afterward to get my oil changed, intending to also be of service to his sales team while there."

"You, serving them. That's an interesting twist."

"I took to heart the message James shared about helping other businesses grow, which, in turn, could help me. So I decided I would refer all the people I know to Doug's sales and service staff. Well, I wasn't there but a couple of minutes when—out of the blue—Cody Gray, one of his sales people, approached me and offered to refer his car buyers my way. What are the odds?"

"Who knows? So were you receptive to Cody's offer?"

"Absolutely! Just as he was with my offer to help him. We even agreed to meet at a café between the dealership and my office to make our introductions."

"Which reminds me, I have a lady I want to introduce you to on Monday afternoon. But I must warn you, the environment where we're meeting could turn into a zoo. Are you up for it?"

"I am. But don't worry. As a former teacher, I'm used to chaos!"

Rolly grinned. "I'll text you the details."

Section 5:
The *I* in S.M.I.L.E.

A Common Thread

When Sherri made the final turn to her destination, she realized where she was going. "Of all places," she said to herself. "We're meeting at the city zoo!"

Having taken classes there on field trips, she recalled a secluded parking lot not far from the entrance. And it was a good thing, as the main parking lot was full of school buses. She made her way to a shaded area of picnic tables where she was to look for a lady in a navy blue jacket.

She approached a lady who met that description. "Excuse me, are you Susan Horton?"

"Yes, and you must be Sherri. It's a pleasure to meet you," Susan responded, giving Sherri a hug. Displaying her cell phone, she continued, "Please forgive me, I'm on hold with Rolly. Let me switch to speaker so we can both hear when he comes back."

Rejoining the call, Rolly spoke up, "Good idea, Susan, and it sounds like Sherri found you. Hello, Sherri, I hope you're okay with it just being you and Susan for now. I had planned to spend the afternoon with both of you. But I was at the table where you are just minutes ago and got swarmed by all the young children. They must have thought I had escaped and were trying to catch me. Normally the zoo is quieter during the week. I apologize."

"I totally understand, Rolly. Your playful warning about this becoming a zoo turned out to be an omen," she teased.

"And that omen had me screaming 'Oh man!' when a little boy tried to grab me by the tail feathers!"

"Oh my! I'm sorry I missed that!"

"Sherri, you won't be sorry about the time you spend with the person who will teach you about the *I* in **S.M.I.L.E.** Since the early 'nineties, Susan has worked in the title, mortgage, new home sales, and property management segments of the industry, becoming a trusted advisor to those she's served. Now she's the managing broker and trainer for John Horton Realty that she and her husband own and operate."

"Impressive credentials!" Sherri said, smiling at Susan.

Rolly agreed. "Susan, I'll leave it up to you to address the topic at hand. Why don't you two spend a few minutes getting to know each other—as if I really need to suggest that—and I'll catch up with you both a little later."

"Sounds good," Susan replied and Sherri nodded.

Putting their phones on Respectful to Both mode in case Rolly called back, the two followed Rolly's suggestion. They were amazed at how much they had in common. After several minutes of fun and laughter, Susan sensed it appropriate to move on to the purpose of their visit. "As you reflect on what you've learned about how to **S.M.I.L.E.**, do you see a common thread connecting the first two letters?"

Sherri pondered the link. "I do, Susan. It's people. The *S* is about keeping it simple for me, as a person, so I can keep it simple for the people I serve. The *M* is about ME, as a person, being responsible for building relationships with the people WE help. And those people, in turn, will help other people."

"You got it! So you're probably wondering, if this is all about people, why are we here at a zoo full of animals?"

"I am a little surprised, Susan."

The Four Behavioral Styles

What shouldn't surprise you is that today is *also* about people. We'll simply use animals to help us better understand people. No pun intended, but are you game?"

"You bet!" Sherri replied as they began strolling through the zoo.

"Sherri, in your real estate training, did you learn about behavioral styles?"

"No, I'm sure I would have remembered that."

"I hadn't either. I knew this business was about people, yet I never received any real training regarding people or about the way they see the world—and the way they behave as a result. I recognized that some guests were a lot like me, but most were different. I just didn't know why. Moreover, I didn't know what to do about it."

"It's interesting you mention that because I easily recognize when someone is a lot like me. We just click. We get along well and conversations flow easily."

"It's as if you're meeting an old friend."

"That's exactly what it's like, Susan. On the flip side, it's also easy to recognize people who are *not* like me. And

depending on how different they are, I may struggle a little—or, in some cases, a lot—when interacting with them. As
a result, I often feel inadequate and frustrated when I can't
relate effectively."

"I'm with you, Sherri! I could easily help those who were
like me but very few who were not. And because there were far
more people who were *not* like me, I felt unprepared to help
most of the people I met—until I met Rolly. When he introduced me to behavioral styles, *everything* changed."

"What did Rolly do?"

Susan had timed their walk perfectly. She stopped and
pointed to the sign over the bird sanctuary.

Welcome to the World

of our Winged Friends

"To help me discover the *I* in **S.M.I.L.E.**, Rolly introduced me to the world of birds."

"I'm intrigued. Do you mind if I take notes?"

"Good idea, Sherri. But I promise we're going to keep this
simple, just as Rolly did for me. We're going to focus on only
four bird families."

"That makes me feel better. If I may ask, what does the *I* in
S.M.I.L.E. represent?"

"Two words share that honor. The *I* stands for Identify the Individual."

I dentify the ndividual

"The first step in identifying the individual is to identify yourself—how *you* see the world. So let's begin with you. Give me a few words that best describe you."

"I'm not used to that, talking about myself."

"So you're somewhat reserved, which is one of the things I like about you, Sherri."

"And I guess I consider myself down-to-earth and easygoing. Doug calls me the 'peacemaker'—I want everyone to get along. He also says I'm caring. I was a schoolteacher, so I'm a good listener and very patient. Plus, I wrote detailed lesson plans that I followed religiously."

"You might write these attributes down as well," Susan suggested. "So you sound like the type of person who will stay on course and probably hasn't changed jobs very often."

"I taught at the same school for twenty years and can be resistant to change. How did you know that?"

"Because people who see the world the way you do *behave* that way. It's a part of their *behavioral* style."

"And you learned that from Rolly?"

"I did. Once you learn the characteristics of the four styles, all you have to do is pay attention to the clues people give you. Those clues will lead you to additional clues that reveal their style. So of all the types of birds we've walked past, is there one in particular that comes to mind that might best represent how you just described yourself?"

As Sherri pondered the question, she noticed Susan had stopped at the dove enclosure. "How did you know to stop here? A dove is precisely what I would have picked."

"Your answers, Sherri. After all, doves are a symbol of peace and love and harmony, which are the essence of you. I'll bet you know a lot of people who remind you of doves."

"I'd say most of the teachers at my school. Now that I picture the image of a dove, it's easy for me to recognize that personality. You've helped me clearly identify myself—and that individual."

"The *I* in **S.M.I.L.E.**, Sherri."

"Wow! I love how simple and visual this is!"

"If you're ready for another, let's try one that's just the opposite." As they resumed their tour of the sanctuary, Susan asked, "Can you recall someone who's very direct, decisive, and at times, confrontational?"

Writing these down, Sherri said, "I'm starting to."

"Someone who is passionate about a task but can also be competitive and strong-willed? A person who is self-confident, is all about results, and needs to be in control?"

"Do you know my husband?" Sherri asked with a big grin. "That is Doug to a tee."

"I'm not at all surprised, Sherri. Have you heard the expression 'opposites attract'?"

"Yes, and Doug and I know we are complete opposites. I hope that's not a bad thing."

"It can be a good thing. To borrow a line from the movie *Jerry Maguire*, you 'complete' each other."

"I can see that. It takes me forever to make decisions, whereas Doug can pull the trigger quickly once he has a command of the facts. Sometimes I need that quality in him, but then there are times he'll need me to talk him down from the ledge when he's not getting the results he expected. I'll remind him to be patient and stay the course."

"I suspect Doug would say that's a good thing, too. So what bird would best represent the Dougs of the world?"

Without hesitating, Sherri retraced her tracks to where the eagles were kept. "My Doug is an Eagle. He's strong, determined, and confident. He won't back down from anything and will stand his ground defending his position."

"You certainly picked the appropriate bird to represent this behavioral style. Do you know any other Eagles?"

"I do. My broker is definitely an Eagle. Like Doug, he's determined and driven to be successful. He challenges us to do our best, and I need that at times."

"Anyone else?"

"My dad is an Eagle. He was an officer in the military and needed those strong leadership qualities to bring out the best in his men. And now that I think about it, my mom is a Dove! Wow, that's ironic. This is fascinating!"

"It is. Are you ready to learn more?"

"You bet, Susan. Which one is next?"

"Let's focus on a very different style from the first two. Do you know someone who is knowledgeable, has a high attention to detail, and wants answers to everything? This person is also very analytical, distrustful of others, and tends to see what's wrong with just about anything."

"I'm almost there, Susan. Give me a few more."

"Someone who is super organized, very precise, and has a high concern for quality."

"You just described Doug's accountant. He is extremely competent, very smart, and great with the books. But on the people side, he is hard to get to know. He questions everything, which in his position can be a good thing. On the other hand, he's a bit of a perfectionist. Those who don't understand him often take him the wrong way. Oh, we had an architect who was like that, too."

"And can you think of a bird for this personality?"

"An owl seems like a logical choice."

"Owls would definitely fit this style. Okay, so let's try the last one."

"I'm ready, Susan. This is fun!"

"Can you think of someone who wants to have fun—at everything. This person is outgoing and charming, is always wearing a smile, and never meets a stranger. Someone who enjoys talking to anybody and everybody, has a positive outlook, and makes others feel good. Finally, this person welcomes personal attention, more than all the other styles combined. Sherri, does this describe anyone you know?"

"I'm blessed to know quite a few like this. Rob Lee, our favorite waiter, came to mind first. Doug and I just love being around him. Oh, and my best friend, Charlene Bueno, too."

As they continued their walk, Susan asked, "Which bird would most appropriately represent this style?"

"We haven't seen them yet, but I know they're here." Looking around, she asked, "Where are the parrots?"

"You're going to love what you're about to discover!"

Turning the corner, Sherri stopped in front of the parrot

aviary—a new addition. Inside, they watched as hundreds flew by, chasing and playing with each other. "Parrots are definitely the bird to represent this style," Susan agreed. "They love to play and have fun and talk. There's never a dull moment around them, that's for sure."

"They remind me of Rolly. I wish he could have been with us this afternoon," Sherri remarked.

"Did I hear someone say they've been missing me?" Rolly asked, landing on a perch behind them.

Sherri and Susan were delighted. "We're so glad you could join us!" Susan exclaimed. "Give us a hug."

"We really did miss you," Sherri added with a big smile. "Did you just get here?"

"After I spoke to you, I decided to drop in here so I could interact with the school children in a more controlled setting. I estimated you would be finishing about now, which is perfect timing since the last school bus just left. This will give us some quiet time to discuss your afternoon."

Combinations of Styles

I t's been eye-opening . . . with a capital *I*!" Sherri said with a wink. "I've had a great time and learned so much from Susan. She really knows her stuff!"

"You're too kind, Sherri. And I love your play on words!" Then addressing Rolly, she continued, "Sherri is so sweet and is such a great listener. You know I love being around Doves since I've got a little Dove in me too."

"Thanks, Susan. Did you say you were part Dove? I took you for a Parrot, just like Rolly."

"You have learned your styles well. I am a Parrot but not *just* a Parrot. I also have a good bit of Dove in me."

"So we can be more than one style?"

"Absolutely," Rolly chimed in. "Unlike we birds that can only be what we are, most humans are actually a combination of two of the styles. Some have three. That's why knowing the characteristics of each style is so important. As you begin to recognize the characteristics of the primary style, you can also look for characteristics of a second or even third style."

Susan added, "And it's that combination, Sherri, that makes us who we are."

"So am I just a Dove?" Sherri asked.

"You're mostly Dove," Rolly stated. "But I see a bit of Parrot in you, too. I see someone who is fun, who can be quite charming, and who is fairly outgoing."

Sherri smiled. "There's a little of you in me, too?"

"Yes, but not as much as Susan," Rolly answered.

"I can see that. Now that I think about it, Doug is not all Eagle. I see some Parrot in him, too. He's almost always smiling, he enjoys talking, and he is quite charming and fun."

"Now you're getting it," Susan encouraged.

"Recognizing the styles of others seems easy. When I relate the four styles to birds, I can readily associate those characteristics. I can easily picture an Eagle, a Parrot, a Dove, and an Owl, or any combination of them in people. But *what* do I do with this information about others?"

"Great question!" Rolly replied. "Once you've identified a person's style, the next step is key. You may need to make adjustments so the interaction is comfortable."

"Sherri, to help you learn the four styles, Rolly asked me to bring you a copy of a diagram we put together. It profiles the four behavioral styles. We hope this helps."

The Four Behavioral Styles

Precise	Direct
Analytical	Decisive
Knowledgeable	Passionate
Super organized	Competitive
Attentive to detail	Strong-willed
Distrustful of others	Self-confident
Concerned about quality	Confrontational
Tends to see what's wrong	Results-oriented
Wants answers to everything	Wants to be in control
Resistant to change	Craves personal interaction
Stays the course	Makes others feel good
Down to earth	Never meets a stranger
Great listener	Positive outlook
Peacemaker	Always smiling
Easygoing	Enjoys talking
Reserved	Outgoing
Patient	Charming
Caring	Fun

"Does it ever! And I love the illustrations of the birds. They make it easy to visualize the four styles."

"That was our goal," Rolly said. "To make it simple."

Comfortable and Uncomfortable

R olly, you mentioned making adjustments to make the interaction comfortable. Could you explain that?"

"Think of each quadrant as the comfort zone for each bird. When a bird interacts with a bird that is like it, things are easy, they're in the same zone, they're comfortable."

"So 'birds of a feather flock together'?"

"They do! Now imagine a bird interacting with a bird from a different quadrant, but the quadrant borders it on the same *side*—right versus left—or the same *level*—upper versus lower. Then the bird will likely experience some discomfort. At the same time, they might also relate with a quality or two that also makes sense to them."

"I can see that. As a Dove, if I'm interacting with an Owl, my resistance to change might appreciate the organized structure and attention to detail that are characteristic of the Owl. If I'm interacting with a Parrot, my strength as a great listener and my easygoing demeanor are a good fit with the Parrot's desire to talk."

"Great examples! Now imagine interacting with a bird in the quadrant that is *diagonally opposite* your own. That's when you will experience the *most* discomfort. To see this, look at the characteristics in the *diagonally opposite* quadrant."

Being a Dove, Sherri scanned the quadrant for the Eagle. "That is so true! My caring and patient nature often conflicts with the direct and in-your-face attitude of the Eagle. At times, they can make me feel most uncomfortable."

Making Adjustments

Now, let's discuss what I mean by making adjustments. Sherri, imagine you are selling birdhouses to birds instead of homes to people."

"That might be fun. My uncle, who's retired, builds birdhouses and sells them at craft fairs."

"There you go, Sherri. Now we know it could happen. So as a Dove with a bit of Parrot mixed in, put yourself in the position of selling birdhouses to each of the four styles. Could you envision being the same with all four styles?"

"Well, I'd like to think my values would always stay the same. But if I wanted to increase my chances of success, I'd do well to treat each style the way *they* want to be treated. If I interact with an Owl the same way I interact with a Parrot, they'd be turned off, and perhaps even offended. And heaven forbid I treat an Eagle like either of the other two! So the only style with whom I could truly be myself would be another Dove."

"Well said!" Susan exclaimed. "We don't change *who we are*, we change *what we do*. Rolly helped me understand that. Unless I'm dealing with my same style, I will need to *behave* differently because of the different *behavioral* styles I encounter. It's our *behavior* that needs to change, not us!"

"Great responses, both of you," Rolly praised. "Now let's tie making adjustments back to comfort zones. Sherri, let's switch from birdhouses to people houses."

"I can make that switch. I wasn't looking forward to competing with my uncle anyway!"

"I'll bet you could give him a run for his money!" Rolly teased. "So if we're in the people business and we build relationships, we understand that those relationships will develop sooner and be stronger if we adjust our behavioral style to operate in our guest's comfort zone."

"This was crucial for me," Susan added. "But to make the adjustment, I had to become comfortable with being uncomfortable. Once I accepted my responsibility to make the adjustment and stepped into *their* comfort zone, my effectiveness improved dramatically."

"Dramatic improvement is an understatement, Sherri. Susan has achieved the distinction of becoming a **Platinum Top 50 Realtor** every year since and just won **Broker of the Year** from her homebuilders association."

"Congratulations, Susan!" Sherri said. "I would love to hear more about the adjustments you made."

"Thank you, Sherri, and you too, Rolly. I'd be happy to share some examples. Just keep in mind, we can't make adjustments until we *Identify* the *Individual*."

"Yes, the *I* in **S.M.I.L.E.**," Rolly concurred. "That's where it all starts. We have to know their behavioral style—it's how they see and interact in the world."

"Let's begin with the Eagles," Susan said. "Once any style identifies they're interacting with Eagles, it's important to give the Eagles a feeling of control while at the same time respectfully standing our ground where our expertise is needed. The key word is *respectfully*. Get to the point and don't ramble with Eagles. As soon as possible, get Eagles talking about their accomplishments. In no time, they will begin to trust us—regardless of our style—to do what we're trained to do. They want to deal with someone they feel is competent."

"I can see all this working for Eagles," Sherri stated.

"As for Parrots—more than any other style—they need to feel important. Compliment them at every turn. They love praise and recognition. And by all means, get them talking about their favorite subject—themselves! Above all, make the experience fun. If we do that, they'll make it fun for us."

"I can picture that working well for Parrots, being part Parrot myself!" Sherri responded with a grin.

"Now to our dear Doves. The biggest adjustment for the other styles is to stop talking and to start listening to the Doves. And the easiest way to do that is to ask questions. The more questions asked, the more the Doves talk, which tells them the other styles care about their opinion and value what they know. Doves appreciate those who exhibit patience, talk slower, and speak in a softer voice. Plus, they value someone who moves the process along, someone who has a plan."

"As a Dove, I can both relate to and appreciate everything you just shared."

"Thanks, Sherri. As for the Owls . . . they want answers. They want information. It's important that what we share is accurate and to the point. Using terms such as 'in the ballpark,' 'close to,' 'about,' or 'trust me' won't work for Owls. And if we don't know the answer to something, we tell them we don't, then tell them we'll get the answer and follow up with them once we have it."

"Would taking notes be important for Owls?"

"All styles appreciate it when you take notes. It says you are listening and that you care. But the owls especially love it! They'll even check to make certain we got everything down. Just don't think it's all business with Owls. Get them talking about where they got their education or their business credentials first. Once they trust you, you can get them to open up about family and travels—the fun things most all of us enjoy about life," Susan emphasized.

"I've noticed that with Doug's accountant," Sherri confirmed. "It just takes a little time with him."

Playing the Percentages

So, Sherri, what are you taking away from today?" Rolly asked. "Learning to identify the individual by applying the *I* in S.M.I.L.E. will help me immensely when dealing with people. I've never been comfortable being uncomfortable. Now I know making adjustments will significantly increase my chances of helping others."

"That sums it up. So let's look at the percentages your chances could increase. Susan, you care to share those?"

"I'd be honored, Rolly. It's estimated that forty percent of the population are Doves. Parrots are second with thirty percent. Eagles come in third with twenty percent. And Owls make up only ten percent."

"This is so helpful!" Sherri realized. "Even though Doves are the largest category, I would naturally struggle with more than half of my guests. And even if I could add in a small portion of me that's Parrot, there are still a lot of guests I would likely be ineffective in trying to help."

"And that's why making adjustments is important, so we can communicate with all of our guests," Susan stressed. "Now you know why the day Rolly introduced me to behavioral styles, my real estate career changed forever."

"Sherri, I know you want to enter notes on what Susan

shared today, so I believe it's best we say our goodbyes so you can get to that."

"Before you go, I want you and Susan to know that what I'm taking away goes far beyond what we've discussed. I feel so blessed to have met you both, as well as everyone else you've introduced me to, Rolly. And I owe somebody a huge debt of gratitude for referring you my way."

"We appreciate your heartfelt words," Susan said.

"What I learned today can be used in every facet of my life. From this day on, I will strive to be more understanding and accepting of how others see the world. I promise to be less judgmental and more compassionate when dealing with others. Simply put, I will be a better version of me."

"So touching, so moving, and spoken like a true Dove!" Rolly declared. Then they all had a good laugh, for Rolly's sense of humor was true Parrot!

A Recipe for Success

Afterward, though, Rolly became unusually pensive. "Everything okay?" Susan broached.

"Did I say something wrong?" Sherri asked.

"I'm more than okay, Susan. Thank you for asking. And, Sherri, you said nothing wrong. In fact, your words were so powerful, they've caused me to rethink my next move in introducing the final two letters in **S.M.I.L.E.**"

"I hope that's a good thing," she replied.

"I believe it's a very good thing, Sherri. With the first three letters, I've controlled when and where they'd be introduced, following the logical order of how they appear in the word. But I want to give you control of the last two."

"I'm honored. What are my options?"

"I've got something occurring tomorrow that's a first. The gentleman who addresses the *E* in **S.M.I.L.E.**, which I had scheduled for next week, happens to be in town *this* week. And I learned this morning that another gentleman, who is every bit his equal, will be here from D.C. tomorrow morning. Since it's rare I ever get them together, we've scheduled a special filming tomorrow. They'll be discussing their sales philosophies and experiences. I think it would be beneficial for you to spend time with both of them."

"Don't tell me Ariff is joining Bert," Susan spoke up. "No way! Those two are rock stars in my book!"

"And I have the privilege of meeting them tomorrow?"

"If you're available and don't mind getting out of order with the letters," Rolly stated.

"Yes, I'm available. And the way I see it, there is no order for the letters. They're more like ingredients in a prize-winning recipe. It doesn't matter which ingredient I start with or end with, as long as I use them all in the appropriate amount. Does that make sense?"

"Does it ever!" Susan remarked. "Rolly, you might want to add a cooking show to tomorrow's taping, starring Sherri. You could call it 'A Recipe for Success.'"

"And after a few more 'cooking classes,' Sherri will be a master chef!" Rolly exclaimed. "We'll start taping at 10 a.m., Sherri. So plan to get there around nine, and we can spend some time together before filming. I'll text you the address."

"I'll be there," Sherri replied. "Susan, will you be joining us tomorrow?"

"I'd give anything to be there, but I've got an entire sales team gathering in the morning to learn what we covered this afternoon. However, please give Ariff and Bert a big hug from me. They are two of the finest men I know!"

Giving Back

'd be glad to," Sherri said. "And, Susan, I don't know why I'm just now realizing this. But you not only do one-on-one training—as you did for me—but you also do training for entire sales teams? I guess the same holds true for James and Sarah and Bob?"

"It does, Sherri. Rolly keeps us—along with an elite list of others who give back—very busy!"

"That sounds rewarding! Rolly, my new goal is to be on your elite list someday. I'd love to help teach others how to S.M.I.L.E., especially Doug's sales team. This would really speak to them."

"Sherri, if you keep holding yourself acCOUNTable, you're guaranteed to make the list!"

She held up her hands and wiggled her fingers. "Then . . . count . . . me . . . in!"

"You got it! Now give us a hug and a smile so I can walk Susan out."

Accountability List—Day 4

Sherri found a quiet place outside the sanctuary to record her thoughts.

Sherri's Accountability List—Day 4

As she reflected on the key elements of the day, many things stood out.

"I need to remind myself every day that not everyone has the same behavioral style as me. And if I just pay attention, they will give me clues to tell me whether they are an Eagle, a Parrot, a Dove, or an Owl, or any combination of the four. I will study the diagram until the styles become second nature."

☐ *Look for the clues of how others see the world.*

"Knowing that most people see things differently from me is one thing, but actually doing something with that knowledge is what matters most. If I want others to be more comfortable around me, it's going to be up to me to make the adjustments—not changing who I am, just what I do."

☐ *Adjust my style to make others feel comfortable.*

Walking to her car, she realized the first three letters of **S.M.I.L.E.** had taught her so much. "I can't wait until tomorrow! This little Dove has so many reasons to be thankful and to smile."

Section 6:
The *E* in S.M.I.L.E.

Noticing Pays Off

"Over here, Sherri. To the side of the stage."

Following the direction of Rolly's voice, Sherri located him on a break table just off camera. "Hello, my friend," she said, offering their customary greeting. "This is a big day for you! I've never rubbed elbows with a real live director. By the way, where's the chair with your name on it?"

"I knew there was something missing. You think I can be as brilliant as Spielberg today?"

"The time is ripe!"

"Which reminds me, thank you for being on time. Unfortunately, Ariff's flight wasn't, so he's still backstage changing, and Bert is getting his microphone attached. While we're waiting, we've got an assortment of beverages. What can I serve you?"

"You're so thoughtful! I'll have the orange juice."

"Orange juice it is. So tell me about your listing appointment."

"It was amazing! I arrived early to put the celebratory champagne on ice and present my housewarming gift—a lovely garden sculpture. I wanted the Carters to know how special they are and how much I appreciated their Quality Introduction. When we went out to find a perfect place for the sculpture, I saw they'd put in a gorgeous swimming pool and spa. It looked like a resort!"

"I'll bet they appreciated the champagne, the gift, and your noticing what they'd done."

"They must have. They're hosting a big party next week and asked if I would come. There are several business owners they want me to meet."

"What an honor and opportunity! So how did the Quality Introduction go?"

"The Carters were so warm and hospitable. Their Quality Introduction set the tone for the rest of the evening. Over dinner, they told their neighbor how impressed they were with my services. What a nice thing to say!"

"They have an eye for talent and a passion for helping."

"Well, they were certainly a help to me. After the celebratory toast, I went next door to the neighbor's home. I could tell she felt comfortable with me when she shared that her husband had passed away recently."

"I'm sorry to hear that. How is she doing?"

"She told me she was adjusting. As she showed me her home, I noticed a picture of Heinz Field in the study. Doug and I watched the Cowboys play the Steelers there, and I easily recognized the stadium because of the bright gold seats. So when I asked if Heinz Field held some special meaning, she showed me several of her husband's photo albums. It turns out he played a major role in the stadium's construction."

"I applaud you again for noticing things!"

"I remembered how important you made me feel when you noticed things in my home. But I noticed more than that. She loved talking—a lot!—which told me she was a Parrot."

"I'm guessing you got the listing?"

"At a very reasonable price. Apparently, she met with two other agents last week, but neither paid any attention to her. All they talked about was their expertise, along with the detailed comps to back up the price they suggested."

"So how did you get it for a lesser amount?"

"In our conversation, she shared she wants to move closer to her only daughter, who's expecting her first child in two months. It's her first grandchild, and she is over the moon with anticipation. When I hugged her—offering my heartfelt congratulations—I thought she'd never let go!"

"You were present for her in that moment—the greatest gift you can give."

"It was a privilege to have her share her upcoming joy with me, along with the unfortunate loss of her husband. As we talked, she mentioned her husband would have wanted her to be with their daughter more than anything. Then she gave me her price and said, 'Let's wrap this up so I can be where I'm needed most!'"

"Good for you, Sherri. And her too!"

"Afterward, she said I was the only one who listened and cared. That brought tears to my eyes."

"Being in the people business and receiving a Quality Introduction establish a solid foundation of trust," Rolly said.

"Well, that trust has led to two calls from agents showing her home today. And get this, each expects to bring me a full price offer by the end of the day. I am so pleased!"

A Wealth of Experience

I am so pleased to meet you, Sherri. My name is Bert Baine and I have the honor, along with Ariff, of helping you learn about the *E* in **S.M.I.L.E.** I've been told you're a hugger."

A man with an infectious smile and a full head of silver hair stood before her. Wearing a long-sleeved shirt and jeans, he possessed a youthful energy and exuded tons of charisma.

"Yes, I'm a hugger. It's a pleasure to meet you, Mr. Baine," Sherri said, leaning in to hug him. Before stepping away, she hugged him again. "The second hug is from Susan Horton. She sends her regards."

"Wow!" Bert exclaimed, shuffling his feet in a dance move. "Two hugs already and the sun's barely up! And, Sherri, you can just call me Bert."

Rolly shook his head. "Sherri, in case you haven't noticed, Bert has more energy than everyone here combined! He lights up a room when he walks in. In fact, we could film this video without floodlights!"

"Without a doubt. And I must say, Bert, your energy is contagious. I don't want to miss a single thing you and Ariff cover today. I'd like permission to take notes, if that's okay?"

"Well, I'm flattered you think what I have to say is worth writing down."

"Don't let him fool you, Sherri," Rolly remarked. "Bert has been selling homes for more than forty years. He's *forgotten* more about sales than most sales people have ever *learned*. A lot of sales people have taken note of his success!"

"Forty years!" Sherri repeated. "That would . . ."

"Make Bert old enough to have sold George Washington his Mount Vernon home," a man quipped. Turning around, Sherri presumed this gentleman with the sharp wit and charming accent was Ariff. Dressed in a suit and tie, he gave a distinguished presence. And his demeanor seemed calm . . . understated.

"And who would have been there when George threw the silver dollar across the Potomac?" Bert jested in response.

"Sherri, I am pleased to introduce Ariff Cassim," Rolly stated. "Ariff, I'd like you to meet Sherri Montgomery."

Sensing Ariff was more formal, Sherri elected to extend her hand. "Sir, it's a privilege to meet you. And I must ask where you're from? Your accent is captivating."

Taking her hand with a gentlemanly bow, Ariff replied, "The pleasure is all mine, Sherri, I assure you. As for my heritage, I'm from Burma, a country in southeast Asia."

"I could listen to you all day. Your voice is so soothing. And before I forget, Susan Horton says hello and asked me to give you a hug."

"I must allow you to fulfill your commitment," he said, extending his arms. "I am honored."

"Sherri, though he doesn't look it either, Ariff surpasses even Bert's forty-plus years in sales," Rolly stated. "How many years is it?"

"Let's just leave it at forty-plus," Ariff said. "As was common in my day and culture, I had to quit school and go to work when I was fourteen."

"When I was fourteen, I was chasing girls!" Bert boasted with a grin.

"Girls were beautiful to behold," Ariff said, "but my father made certain my focus was on a career. Being a distributer to the local mercantile stores, he secured a job for me selling textiles. Though small and family-owned, the store outsold all the others my father called on. He requested the wife, who handled sales, to take me under her wing."

"That's not a bad place to be, if I do say so myself," Rolly remarked, spreading his wings.

"I agree, Rolly," Sherri giggled. "And judging from your success, Ariff, she must have taught you well."

"Thank you, Sherri. Yes, she taught me about sales, and I am forever grateful for that. But, more importantly, she taught me about life. The way she chose to live each day was inspirational. Through her actions, she modeled how to *enjoy . . . everyone* we meet and *everything* we do . . . the *E* in **S.M.I.L.E.** And this lesson has forever shaped my life."

ENJOY

Sherri was moved by the purity and power of his words.

ENJOY *everyone and everything*

"That's a refreshing way to approach each day," she said. "A refreshing approach to *life!*"

"It is, Sherri. So let's break this down. I'm certain Rolly has helped you recognize the importance of being in the *people* business . . . in putting *people* first."

"Yes, between Rolly and everyone else, I now see how important that is."

"Very good! When we choose to *enjoy* everyone we meet—the people part of what we do—we not only fall in love with them, we also fall in love with the things we do, both *for* and *with* them. Those *things* become dear to us and enable us to connect with them . . . to understand them . . . to better serve them."

"That was certainly the case when I was a teacher. I loved my students and, therefore, loved teaching."

"That doesn't surprise me. As the saying goes, 'When you love what you do, you never have to work a day in your life.'"

"I *love* that expression!"

"And it's so true," Ariff stated. "Since I love what I do, I have theoretically never worked a day in my life. And if that doesn't put a smile on your face, nothing will!"

"Is it the same for you, Bert?" Sherri asked.

"Definitely!" Bert agreed. "I see my 'workplace' as my 'playground' and the guests who come to see me as new kids joining me in my sandbox. I want the buying experience to be fun."

"I have no doubt you make it fun," Sherri said. "And I love your choice of words. Envisioning your workplace as your playground reminds me of Pike Place Fish Market in Seattle. There the workers don't just sell fish; they make the experience entertaining. When Doug and I went there, we watched the guys throw fish to each other while laughing and joking with their guests. They seemed to truly enjoy every aspect of being in the *people* business."

"I would love to see that!" Ariff remarked.

"You should," she recommended. "Like Bert's vision, the fish market was a playground and the guests were like kids. Everyone had a blast together, buying and selling fish!"

Rules of Shopping 1 & 7

Though the notion of enjoying is the *last* letter of S.M.I.L.E.," Ariff said, "it's also the message of Rolly's **1st Rule of Shopping**:

We're just big kids . . . with more money.

"Pardon the pun, but Rolly's first rule is 'on the money,'" Bert said. "If I had fifty cents when I was a kid, I couldn't wait to spend it. My dad would say that money was 'burning a hole in my pocket.' And it still does . . . it's just much more than fifty cents now."

"I can totally relate," Sherri remarked. "When I was young, it was so much fun to buy a five-dollar toy from the allowance I'd saved. By college, I would gladly spend fifty dollars on a concert ticket to see my favorite band. Now Doug and I will spend five hundred dollars on the newest version of our cell phone."

"So, if you notice, Sherri, the only thing that has changed over the years is the decimal point," Ariff said. "And it's the same for me. When I moved to this country, I recall being so excited to buy a car for five thousand dollars. And I wasted gallons of gas driving it around just for fun. Now I shell out fifty thousand dollars for a new car to get that same feeling."

"Rolly is right," Sherri decided. "We're still kids with a little more money to spend. And we want *spending* it to be *fun!*"

"Though some might not want to admit it," Ariff added, "we still have 'a kid' inside of us. This childlike side reminds us how important it is to have fun . . . to laugh . . . and to enjoy life."

"When a sales person understands the importance of this childlike enthusiasm and makes shopping fun, he or she will make it easy for us to feel good about the *experience*," Bert explained.

Ariff nodded. "This *experience* Bert just mentioned brings us to Rolly's **7th Rule of Shopping**:

We will tell others about our experience.

"Which ties into all the referrals both James Smothers and John Norris received from the families who were so pleased with their experience," Sherri pointed out.

"Very good!" Rolly chimed in.

"Thanks, Rolly. To me, the first and seventh rules almost serve as bookends for the others. The first sets the tone for creating an extraordinary experience. Then the seventh reminds us that when we create an extraordinary experience, the process will be recreated with the person referred to us."

In Our Own Way

Let's get back to the *E* in **S.M.I.L.E.**," Ariff suggested. "According to the dictionary, *enjoy* means 'to have a good experience.' Another interpretation is 'to have a good time.' For Bert, you might expect enjoyment to manifest itself through playing, laughing, joking around . . . simply having a good time. He's jovial and always cutting up with people."

"That's what I experienced with Rolly," Sherri said. "He made our time together so much fun. In fact, 'have more fun' was the first reminder on my Accountability List for Day 1. It was that important to me."

"So Bert and Rolly tend to use humor to create an enjoyable

experience," Ariff reiterated. "For me, enjoyment is creating a pleasant and welcoming environment, 'a good experience,' as the definition states. I have fun with my guests but with a more mellow approach."

"And your approach is just right for you," Bert stated. "It works every bit as well as Rolly's does for him or mine for me. The key is to enjoy *everyone we meet* and *everything we do* . . . in *our own way*."

"I should have the cameras rolling," Rolly called out. "Can you guys remember all this when we start filming?"

"We'll do our best," Ariff replied, bowing his head slightly and clasping his hands respectfully.

"Probably not," Bert said flippantly, flailing his arms. "We're making this stuff up as we go."

Everyone laughed. Then Rolly spoke up. "Sherri, what these two are telling you—and, more importantly, showing you—is that you can enjoy everyone and everything in your own way . . . while being *you*."

"I clearly see where each is coming from. Bert is all Parrot, so his way of enjoying people is to get them laughing by joking around."

"I will own that description!" Bert declared as he high-fived Sherri.

"That's so you. No wonder people enjoy referring their friends and family to you."

"Of course, you realize I can't be that way all the time or with everyone," Bert added. "When I'm with an Owl, I dial it back. I may have to be quite serious with them until they're ready to lighten up. But make no mistake, I'll go from formal to fun as soon as I have the green light!"

Addressing Ariff, Sherri continued, "And, Ariff, you must be the purest Dove I've ever met. Your pleasant and welcoming demeanor is your way of enjoying people. And they are drawn to you and recognize your sincerity. You remind me of Mr. Rogers from the TV show. Every day is 'a beautiful day in the neighborhood.' And I'd live in your neighborhood *any* day!"

"Now I know what I'm getting Ariff for Christmas," Bert exclaimed. "A zip-up cardigan!"

"And I'll get you a red rubber ball for your nose like Robin Williams wore in *Patch Adams!*"

This time everyone roared. "On that high note, I think it's high time we get started," Rolly suggested. "Sherri, I have a few things to go over with these two before filming. You're more than welcome to stay and watch and then join us afterward for lunch."

"Thank you, Rolly. I'll take this opportunity to jot down a few additional notes and check my messages. In case I get 'lucky' and have an offer—or two—to present on the home, it might be wise to say our goodbyes now. That way, I can just slip out. Is that okay?"

"More than okay. I have a hunch you'll be lucky. Let's plan on meeting Friday morning to introduce you to the *L* in S.M.I.L.E. I'll text you the details this evening."

"By the way, Sherri, you'll love learning about the *L*," Ariff stated. "It's especially helpful for us Doves."

"It's important for us Parrots, too!" Bert chimed in. "But most of all, it's important for our guests. They benefit from it as much—if not more—than we do!"

"With that endorsement, I can hardly wait!"

As Rolly walked Bert and Ariff to the set, Sherri took a seat near the exit and checked her messages. A text alerted her that she would receive a contract by lunch with an above-price offer on the home. "I can't wait to present the offer," she thought. "Since meeting Rolly, I am *enjoying everyone* I meet and *everything* I do!" She smiled, knowing she was already living the *E* in **S.M.I.L.E.**

Accountability List—Day 5

Sherri quickly turned to the page in her notepad where she had written

Sherri's Accountability List—Day 5

Without hesitation, she recorded what might be the most important message of any of the letters in **S.M.I.L.E.**

☐ *Enjoy everyone . . . and everything!*

Watching Bert and Ariff offstage, she couldn't help but notice their interaction. They were smiling, laughing, and enjoying what they were doing. They were living proof of Rolly's **1st Rule of Shopping**. "They're just big kids with more money," she said to herself. Then Rolly introduced Bert and Ariff, sharing that together they had sold more than one billion dollars in real estate. "Wow!" she thought, watching them walk out. "They're just big kids with *a lot* more money!"

Both Bert and Ariff shared story after story about the difference they had had the privilege of making in the lives of others. And Sherri recognized their focus had been on *outcome* rather than *income*. They were walking, talking proof of what they had just taught her. They more than enjoyed what they were doing . . . they *loved* it. "If I can enjoy everyone I meet and everything I do, I'll never have to work another day!"

☐ *Love what you do, and you can retire today!*

Sherri decided to stay and listen when she heard Rolly ask Bert and Ariff to describe one thing they did that separated them from everybody else. "I've got to stick around for this!" she thought.

The P Paradox

Bert spoke first. "*Time* is the difference. People are smart enough to know when they're being sold, so I try not to be stupid. I put as much time as I can between when we meet and when we start talking about what I have to sell."

Rolly clarified, "So you're saying the more time you put between person and product, the more they want to buy?"

"Precisely! I wait for the people to start talking about the product. I don't bring it up. They notice that and they love it. The less I try to sell, the more they want to buy!"

"I witnessed the same thing half a world away," Ariff stated. "The person who taught me how to sell would do the same. She called it the **P Paradox**. The more time she focused on the **P**erson and the less time she talked about the **P**roduct . . . in no time her guests wanted to **P**urchase. It helped her enjoy everyone and everything!"

"I like that!" Bert exclaimed. "She was a smart woman!"

"That she was," Ariff agreed. "She was smart enough to know her knowledge of her product wasn't what was most important to the people coming into her store. What *was* important was how she made them feel during their time there. She would constantly remind me that they didn't *care* how much she *knew* until they *knew* how much she *cared*."

"That's a Zig Ziglar quote, isn't it?" Bert asked.

"He often gets credit, but Theodore Roosevelt may have said it first. Regardless, the message is timeless and universal. And my boss practiced what she preached every day by thanking people for coming in, even if they were just asking for directions. She would treat them like a guest in her home, insisting they join her for a cup of tea. Only when they noticed something in her store or mentioned what they were looking for would she talk about her product. Practicing the **P Paradox**, she outsold her competitors ten to one."

"That's fascinating," Bert remarked. "I'll bet our viewers would be equally fascinated in hearing the story of how you came to America and ended up in real estate. Would you mind sharing that? It's one of my favorites."

Sherri noticed the shift in Ariff's demeanor when asked to talk about himself. After all, the story he had just shared was not about him. It was about his mentor, the woman who trained him. "If you feel it will help others," he replied, tugging on the sleeves of his suit coat.

As a Dove, Sherri appreciated Ariff's modesty. But she was equally impressed with Bert. Most Parrots prefer to be the center of attention. But Bert showed humility, offering Ariff the spotlight. "The Parrot in me needs to remember that," she said to herself. "Make others the star of the show."

"When I came to this country, I accepted a position at the biggest furniture store in our nation's capital," Ariff began. "Since I had no formal sales training in the U.S. and wasn't fluent in English, I did all the behind-the-scenes work. I cleaned, I stocked, I did inventory . . . and I was fine with that. I had to pay my dues. And because I enjoyed everyone I was around and everything I did, I loved it! The *E* in **S.M.I.L.E.** makes us grateful for everyone and everything. It's an attitude of gratitude that my first boss taught me and my new bosses noticed and appreciated."

"That it does, my friend," Bert said. "So tell them about your big break. This is the best part!"

"One holiday weekend, we were short several sales people in the furniture department, so they asked me to fill in. I didn't know anything about furniture, but I knew people, so I practiced the **P Paradox**. I put as much time as I could between people—what I knew—and furniture—what I didn't know. The result? I outsold everyone that day."

"And the next . . . and the next!" Bert added.

"I got lucky, my friend."

"As I recall, that luck continued when they moved you to the floor-coverings department."

"Again, I knew nothing about floor coverings, so I put as much time as I could between people—what I knew—and floor coverings—what I didn't know. And outsold everyone."

"If I'm not mistaken, by practicing the **P Paradox** you became their top sales person ever!"

"I don't know about *ever*," Ariff stated humbly. "But I was the top one for all the years I was there."

Rolly chose to get in on the fun. "Then Ariff decided to get into real estate. Again, he practiced the **P Paradox**—enjoying everyone and everything—and became the top sales person for one of the nation's largest homebuilders!"

Accountability List—Day 5 *(Continued)*

As the discussion continued, Sherri discreetly slipped out to her car. "Rolly, Bob, Sarah, James, John, Susan, Bert, and Ariff are all sharing the same message," she realized. "And today that message became crystal clear. Little by little . . . one by one . . . letter by letter . . . **S.M.I.L.E.** is all about people *and* relationships. And the time we spend with others *as* people is what develops those relationships."

The **P Paradox** helped drive that message home for Sherri. "The more time you focus on the **P**erson and the less time you talk about your **P**roduct, in no time your guests will *want* to **P**urchase. It ensures you will enjoy everyone and everything!"

☐ *Practicing the P Paradox ensures I will enjoy everyone and everything!*

Checking her makeup in the visor mirror, she couldn't help but notice she was smiling. "The smile I'm most looking forward to seeing will be that of the Carters' neighbor when I share the great news on the offer! I can't wait!"

A Happy Ending

Thank you for agreeing to meet me here for breakfast, Sherri. Horseshoe Bay is one of my favorite resorts," Rolly said, extending his wings for their customary hug.

"I can see why, Rolly. It looks like a setting from a movie. Which reminds me, how was your filming?"

"A huge success, and I'm anxious to see the finished product. Thank you for asking. But I'm more anxious to learn about you and your success. How have you been?"

"I've been busy! I was able to reconnect with another couple I met just after I got my license. Along with everything else I've learned, I applied the **P Paradox,** and wouldn't you know it, they purchased a home I showed them yesterday. After my time with Bert and Ariff, I've learned to enjoy everyone and everything. I am most blessed!"

"Congratulations! Your success is much deserved. And I'm certain that family recognized just how special you are. Today I'm introducing you to another special person. His name is Christophe, and he reserved this table by the window so we can enjoy the view. And he made freshly squeezed orange juice . . . just for you," Rolly indicated the glass in front of her.

"How thoughtful!" she said. "How did he know that's what I liked?"

"He asked. As you'll soon discover, he's all about service and making others feel important. In the meantime, tell me about the offers you were expecting on your listing."

"We received two, well above the listing price. The owner chose to accept the cash offer with no contingencies. It came with a hefty earnest money deposit, and we'll be closing in ten days. When she called her daughter with the good news, we all just bawled!"

"That is touching."

"It gets better, Rolly! She shared that she still had her daughter's crib from when she was an infant. She wanted to take it to her as a surprise but was concerned about the high mileage on her car. When her husband was sick, they had postponed buying a new car because of his medical expenses."

"I get the feeling there's a happy ending to this story."

"There is! Having just received a check on his life insurance and feeling comfortable with the cash offer, she is en route this very minute to set up the crib tonight, driving a new vehicle from Doug's dealership!"

"Did you have anything to do with that?"

"Maybe," Sherri grinned. "She followed me to the café where Cody and I agreed to meet for our Quality Introductions. Well, you can imagine the rest of the story."

"Wow! Based on two Quality Introductions—the Carters to their neighbor and her to Cody—and your holding yourself acCOUNTable, everyone's happy!"

"Extremely happy! The only thing that would make me any happier is to give you a Quality Introduction to Doug's team when I've earned the right to teach **S.M.I.L.E.** Though they're doing better than ever, I'd love to help them any way I can."

"After Christophe shares the *L* in **S.M.I.L.E.**, we might have to consider that."

Section 7:
The *L* in S.M.I.L.E.

An Opportunity

I heard someone mention my name. Are you talking about me again?" asked a man with a charming European accent.

"That I was!" Rolly answered. "Sherri, I'd like you to meet Christophe Hardenne. Christophe, this is Sherri Montgomery."

Sherri graciously accepted Christophe's offer for a hug. "Rolly, is this the same Christophe who introduced you to Joe Brown?"

"It is. I'm impressed you remembered that!"

"We Doves are good listeners," she said with a wink. "It's a pleasure to meet you, Christophe. And thank you so much for the fresh orange juice."

"The pleasure is all mine . . . both meeting you and serving you, Sherri," he replied, pronouncing her name share-REE.

"I love your accent. May I ask where you're from?"

"Detroit," he teased. "Actually, I was born and raised in Belgium. But I got to America as quickly as I could."

"Cute! So what brought you here from Detroit?" Sherri playfully responded.

"Sherri, I came to America for the opportunities. I love people. And I believe this country is one of the few places where if you care about people—if you treat them well and if you're willing to work hard *and* smart—you can truly be rewarded. I just stayed focused on that belief and everything took care of itself."

"I'd say so," Rolly responded. "In no time, Christophe began working his way up the corporate ladder in the hospitality industry, eventually becoming the director of food and beverage here, where he managed a team of more than 270 employees. He's now an associate with a high-end custom builder in the area. Thanks to Christophe's efforts, not only have their margins increased significantly, but their sales have skyrocketed. Their biggest challenge now is building all the homes he's selling!"

Little Decisions

I am so blessed. And I truly appreciate the kind words," Christophe said. "It's interesting you reference our *biggest* challenge because it was the *little* things you taught me about how to **S.M.I.L.E.** that made the biggest difference for me."

"You phrased that so beautifully!" Sherri exclaimed. "May I write that down?"

"I would be honored. I'm just curious if you will spell the words the correct way or the way I pronounce them?"

"If I thought they'd sound half as charming when I say them, I'd spell them your way!"

They laughed. "Did your emphasis on the word *little* in any way relate to the *L* in **S.M.I.L.E.**?" she asked.

"That's phenomenal, Sherri! Yes, the *L* reminds us that the little decisions simplify the bigger ones. This helped take the fear out of buying for my guests and made it easier for them to say yes."

LITTLE *decisions simplify the bigger ones!*

"I can already tell I'm going to love this one too. I love any-thing that will make it easier for people to say yes. How do you apply it to homebuilding?"

"Good question. Rolly told me you recently got into real estate. As you likely know, the decision to purchase a home can seem overwhelming. It's the biggest financial decision many will ever make. It can be haunting!" Then questioning his word choice, he restated, "No . . . I mean daunting . . . it can be daunting. Forgive me. I still struggle with your language."

"Actually, Christophe, your statement might be very appropriate," Sherri remarked. "If you think about it, the decision to buy a home can be scary. So it could be both haunting . . . and daunting."

"Either way, the *L* in **S.M.I.L.E.** is intended to help our guests understand that buying a home—new or resale—is not one big decision but a series of little decisions."

"I like the way that sounds. Can you elaborate?"

"If I knew what *elaborate* meant . . ." Christophe smiled, shrugging his shoulders.

"Please forgive me. It means to explain . . . to go into detail . . . to give an example. Let's try this. Pretend I'm a potential home buyer and you ask me the questions as if I were your guest. Does that work?"

"Absolutely!" Christophe replied. "Elaborate, I don't under-stand. Example, I do."

"Thank you for making this so much fun."

"To me, I'm just Christophe. Here goes. I would first begin by asking you, 'Sherri, have you ever purchased or built a new home before?'"

"I've never *built* a home, but I have *purchased* one."

"For my response, I need to borrow your pen and notepad. I'll write these down just as I would if you were shopping for a home from me."

She offered her pen and notepad.

"Then you're aware, Sherri, that the decision to buy a home is not one *big* decision but a series of *little* decisions. For example, there's the home, the property or homesite it's on, and the neighborhood it's in. Nearby schools may be a consideration, location-location-location we know is important, as well as convenience to shopping."

☐ Home

☐ Property / Homesite

☐ Neighborhood

☐ Schools

☐ Location

☐ Shopping

"Of these choices, Sherri, where would you like to begin?"

Sherri sat in silence.

"You okay, Sherri? Do I need to refresh your drink?"

"I'm fine, Christophe. That is, if being in shock is fine. This is brilliant, simply brilliant. It not only makes the decision process simple for my guests—back to the *S* in **S.M.I.L.E.**—but because it's written down, it's visual. This makes it all the more powerful!"

"I'm glad you recognize its importance. Now let's see if there's something more profound to which we can relate."

As Sherri studied what Christophe had written, it suddenly came to her. "We have a checklist, which is how most of us function in the world. We make a list, and then we prioritize the items—and our goal is to check things off. Why haven't I thought of that?"

"I asked myself that exact question, Sherri. That's the part about working smart I had to learn. Now let's see if you were paying attention. After the list is made, what's the value in my question that followed?"

"Your question of where I'd like to begin tells you what I feel is the most important thing on that list. It starts the process of prioritizing. And if you are successful at getting a yes to the first thing, I'm guessing you would repeat the same question for the remaining items."

"Precisely! It's like a snowball on a mountain slope. The first yes gets it started downhill. And with each little yes that follows, it builds momentum until it's almost unstoppable."

Stay Focused

Let's see if we can make it even simpler. If your answer to my initial question of where to begin is 'neighborhood,' I would circle that word"—Christophe did so—"and thank you for sharing your answer."

☐ Home

☐ Property / Homesite

☒ (Neighborhood)

☐ Schools

☐ Location

☐ Shopping

"Then I'd ask you to describe the neighborhood you live in now. Then—"

"I think I know where you're going," Sherri interjected. "Then you'd want to know three things: what I LIKE about my neighborhood, what I DISLIKE about it, and what I'd CHANGE about it if I could.

Flipping back to Bob's drawing, she continued, "And you'd simply lay them out on a page in a landscape position . . . just like this."

"Rolly, you've taught her well!"

"Actually, Bob helped her with this," Rolly said. "Sherri, if I might ask, what is Christophe's purpose in circling your answer?"

"I'm thinking it's to have me focus . . . to draw my eyes to just that one topic, like a target or bull's-eye."

"Exactly! Drawing our eyes to it allows us to concentrate on that specific item. So circling it *eye*-solates that little decision," Christophe emphasized, pointing to his eye. "You like that, Rolly?"

"Very clever," he replied. "By the way, you did a great job elaborating on that!"

"Thank you. I try to learn something new every day."

"Me, too!" Sherri chimed in. "I see now that your very first question—whether I had built or purchased a home before—is engaging. It's designed to draw the person into the conversation, making them curious as to why you asked."

"That's the purpose," Rolly said.

Rules of Shopping 5 & 6

Sherri paused a moment, deep in thought. "Rolly, after I ask about the home they HAVE NOW—and the three questions that follow—I could respond to my guest's answers with Christophe's question, 'Did you purchase this new or did you have it built?' And that, in turn, sets the stage to make the checklist to discuss the little decisions. This is so powerful I'm surprised it's not one of your Rules of Shopping."

Christophe was astonished. "Are you kidding me, Sherri? It *is* his **5th Rule of Shopping**:

Little decisions help simplify the bigger ones.

"It does make sense though because it relates directly to the *S* in **S.M.I.L.E.**," Sherri mused. "It's about keeping it SIMPLE . . . for me and for my guests. So the 6th Rule is the only one that's missing. I imagine it's somehow connected with this one."

"It is, Sherri. When folks come to see you or me, they're hoping to improve their situation—whatever's going on in their world that has them searching for something better than what they HAVE NOW. So think about this: If we have helped them create this checklist of little decisions and together we've put check marks beside the important ones, what *has* to happen for their situation to improve?"

"That's easy. They *have* to buy!"

"But what if they *don't* buy?"

"Then their situation *hasn't* improved."

"Which is Rolly's **6th Rule of Shopping**:

Until we buy, our situation has not improved.

"I realize all the questions Bob helped me with are on your list of little decisions," Sherri said. "And being on paper—for all to see—allows me to lead them to the only decision that makes sense, one they *have* to make if they are honest with themselves about wanting their situation to improve."

"You got it. And the check marks make the decision *easy* to make so their situation *can* improve."

Checklists Are Key

Simple yet profound," Sherri uttered. "This checklist of little decisions really becomes our to-do list that guides us and our guests through the entire process. It is the easiest way to help them say yes! I love it! I love what I do! I love to smile! I *love* S.M.I.L.E.! And I can't wait to start applying this letter, too!"

Christophe turned to Rolly. "I *think* she's learned how to S.M.I.L.E. You agree?"

"Oh, she's *definitely* got it."

"You know, you did more than fill a pail," Sherri said tearfully. "You lit a *fire* in me. And I thank you and Christophe and all the others."

"That reminds me . . . anyone hungry for a hot breakfast?" Christophe inquired.

"I'm hungry for two things," Sherri responded. "Breakfast *and* an answer. This Sunday I will have known Rolly for two weeks . . . long enough to know there's a reason behind everything he does. I'm curious why we met here?"

"We can't pull the sweater over her eyes!" Christophe said to Rolly.

Sherri and Rolly burst out laughing. "Is it something I said?" Christophe questioned with a perplexed look on his face.

"It's 'pull the *wool* over her eyes,'" Rolly replied, trying to regain his composure. "The *wool* . . . not the sweater. It's kind of the same . . . but different."

"Now I've learned two things today," Christophe declared. "This is a *phenomenal* day!"

"We chose to meet here for two reasons," Rolly explained. "The first is so you can experience Christophe's servant heart. In a few minutes you're about to enjoy the best breakfast ever, prepared and served by Christophe himself."

"What an honor. I can hardly wait!" Sherri rejoiced.

"The honor is *mine*, I assure you," Christophe stated. "The second reason, Sherri, involves a reminder. I understand your husband, Doug, owns a car dealership. I am curious if you have attended any of the corporate events put on by the car manufacturers?"

"Yes, I've been to several."

"The next one you attend, or the next hotel or conference center you drive by that is holding a large event, I want you to remember that the decision to book a hotel or conference center involves someone being comfortable saying yes. Yes to what? For starters, the meeting space. A room large enough to accommodate everyone and everything is always a top priority. And because there will likely be visual presentations, audio/visual considerations will also be needed."

"Those are important."

"Also, since most attending are likely from out of town, they will need sleeping rooms. Plus, amenities such as a pool, gym, spa, salon, and tennis courts may be important. Let's not forget about transportation to and from the airport or to outside venues that might be involved." Gesturing to where they are now, Christophe continued, "And since these folks will likely get hungry at some point, food and beverage will be another important element. You see what I mean, Sherri?"

"I never really thought of the scope of something that big. I would feel overwhelmed trying to make that decision."

"Or would you? Think about it for a moment."

Sherri reconsidered based on what she'd just learned. "Not if the person taking me through the property helped me create a checklist of all the little decisions. Then it would be doable—one little decision at a time—from a checklist."

"You got it. So, one final question. What's the likelihood any hotel or conference center would have *exactly* what that company was searching for in *every* department or area?"

"Exactly? In every area? I'd say rare, if ever."

"Based on my twenty-three years in hospitality, I'd say

you're correct. A perfect match almost *never* happens. Yet bookings are made every minute of every day everywhere across the world. So how do you explain that?"

"Because it's only necessary to say yes to the most *important* little decisions," she concluded. "And the key to knowing those . . . is the checklist. I would imagine that holds true for real estate. Finding a home or property that meets *every* little requirement is unlikely. But finding the one that satisfies the most important ones is doable if we create our checklist."

"That's beautiful!" Christophe responded.

"And the real beauty is that it likely works in just about any industry," Sherri said. "We know it works for homebuilding, real estate, and hospitality." She turned to Rolly. "It obviously works for swimming pools since you're now teaching that industry how to **S.M.I.L.E.**" With a grin, she added, "I'll bet it can also work for the automotive industry. Am I right?"

"I guess we'll just have to find out."

Carpe Diem

If you will excuse me, Sherri, I will be back in a moment to begin serving you," Christophe said.

"And what about Rolly?"

"I told Christophe earlier that I need to forgo breakfast," Rolly explained. "I have two appointments today."

"Rolly, you are the busiest parrot I know!" Sherri teased. "Can we assume that both are referrals?"

"Only the first, which involves lunch with the owners of Crescent House Furniture, who I'm super excited to meet. This afternoon's visit is with Harry Roberts, one of the founders of Mattress Firm, along with his brother Charlie, who is his business partner. I'm hoping I can be of help to both organizations."

Christophe was intrigued. "I'm curious, if Mattress Firm wasn't a referral, how did you meet those folks?"

"On a dinner cruise. Gwen and I met Charlie and his wife, Sue, and started visiting with them—what they do for fun and work, where they're from, past careers, how they met."

Sherri couldn't help but interrupt. "You pretended you saw the sign hanging around each of their necks!"

"How could I miss them? After all, everyone is wearing one. The next thing I know, Charlie expressed an interest in what I do, and we discussed **S.M.I.L.E.** It was a fun visit. And that visit led to this afternoon's visit."

"And as Christophe so eloquently stated, 'If you care about people, if you treat them well, and if you're willing to work hard *and* smart, you can truly be rewarded for it.' You've just changed the 'work hard' part to 'play hard' since you enjoy everyone you meet and everything you do," Sherri said.

"The *E* in **S.M.I.L.E.** Picture that!" Christophe added.

"And pictures are just what I'd like to see, Rolly. Did you happen to take any of the cruise?"

"Thank you for asking, Sherri. Check these out!"

Sherri and Christophe admired the photos on his phone. "Rolly, if all goes well—as I'm certain it will—I'd love to meet with both organizations, as well as the folks with the pool company you're helping. I can give them lots of Quality Introductions since the families I help might need new bedding for sleeping . . . or a new pool for swimming . . . or furniture for their home. The world is full of opportunities to help others!"

"Carpe diem, Sherri! You seized the day asking for a Quality Introduction."

"I may be a meek little Dove, but I can be as quick as you Parrots any day!" she replied, flapping her arms. "I'm small and agile."

"I love this lady! She's the best!" Christophe declared. "And yes, Sherri, I am a Parrot, combined with a little Eagle and Dove. And I plan to give you Quality Introductions to guests for whom my homes don't work or who have homes of their own they need to sell. If your schedule permits, why don't you follow me to my neighborhood after breakfast. I'd like to show you my sandbox where—like Bert—I get to enjoy my time with my guests."

"I will gladly accept your offer, Christophe. And I intend to bring you more guests than you can shake a stick at who might be interested in building a new home."

"I would be honored, Sherri. But why would I want to shake a stick at them? I don't want to scare them. I want to make them smile."

Sherri and Rolly enjoyed another laugh. "It's my turn to explain the expression, Rolly. That way, you can leave for your meeting."

Rolly gave them both a farewell hug. "Sherri, you keep holding yourself acCOUNTable. And, Christophe, thank you for your hospitality. Both of you, keep smiling! I'll be in touch before the weekend is over."

Accountability List—Day 6

Sherri walked Rolly out, taking a few minutes to enjoy the scenery and the boats on the lake. Returning to the table, she discovered the most appetizing tray of freshly sliced pineapple, kiwi, cantaloupe, and watermelon. Fresh strawberries, blueberries, and blackberries lined the edge. Her glass of orange juice was refreshed, and a glass of milk and a cup of coffee were poured. Silverware was carefully arranged on either side of a porcelain plate adorned with the most beautiful red rose and a handwritten note on linen stationery.

Sherri,
I will return in a
moment to serve you.

Please enjoy!
Christophe

"How elegant," she thought. "Rolly set the bar high, and Christophe has already exceeded it. I love this!"

Taking out her notepad, she turned to her final list:

Sherri's Accountability List—Day 6

"To me, the *L* in **S.M.I.L.E.** takes the *S* to another level of simplicity," she thought. "My guests will be relieved when the big decision they're considering is reduced to a series of little decisions."

☐ *Little is BIG!*

"And what makes it so big is we create a checklist—on paper—that they can easily visualize."

☐ *A checklist—on paper—is the key.*

Sherri recalled a video that claimed the attention span of the average adult is one second less than a goldfish. "My circling their little decisions one by one will help keep their attention focused. That's a *must-do* on my list."

☐ *Circle their answers. Focus on one at a time.*

"Rolly's **6th Rule of Shopping** really hit home. When a guest knows a decision is right and it's time to say yes, I *have* to help them get there. It comes down to past versus future. If they want to improve their past situation, they must say yes to enjoy their future situation."

☐ *YES is their answer to a better future.*

"The beauty of the checklist of little decisions is that I can help them get to the yes by simply pointing out all the checkmarks they've made. Because these are *their* answers—and they're *written down*—they can't argue with them."

A Testament to Character

For the next hour, Sherri enjoyed the most delightful breakfast. The meal was absolutely delicious; the service, exquisite. "If Belgium has a royal family," she told Christophe, "you have made me queen for the day!"

Their conversation was relaxed and natural, covering everything under the sun—the little things that both knew were actually big things. Sherri learned about Christophe's wife, Priscilla, and their two sons. And her explanation of "to shake a stick at" offered just the perfect touch of humor.

What she enjoyed most was Christophe. He was a living, breathing testament to Bob's sign. His thoughts, words, actions, and habits came to life in his character. He loved life, he loved people, and he loved putting others first. She knew people were drawn to him because of who he was as a person. She hoped others would be drawn to her for the same reason. "**S.M.I.L.E.** is as much about *who* you are as it is about *what* you do," she thought. "Rolly said it best: 'The most important thing you have to offer—the most important thing you're selling—is *you*.' **S.M.I.L.E.** simply brings out the best of who I can be!"

As they headed to Christophe's neighborhood, both knew they had found a lifelong friend.

People Helping People

Fancy getting a call from you on this gorgeous Sunday afternoon," Sherri said. "To what do I owe this pleasure, Mr. Rolly?"

"I thought I'd drop by to say hello on our two-week anniversary," he replied.

"It has been two weeks, hasn't it? And you said 'drop by.' Are you . . . nearby?"

"If you consider your back patio 'nearby.'"

Glancing out the door, she saw Rolly perched on the arm of the loveseat. She immediately rushed out to give him the biggest hug ever. "Your ears must have been burning! I was just on the phone with Linda Carter talking about you."

"She and her husband were the first to buy from you and then referred their neighbor, right? And you were discussing little old me because . . ."

"Because I'd like to introduce little old you to Linda. She's the CEO of Life's Next Step. They help downsize folks—mostly seniors—into more practical surroundings. She does her best to put a smile on their faces and is putting a smile on mine by referring me to families and businesses who could use my help."

"Sounds worthwhile, and congrats on the referrals. James and John would be proud of the relationships you're building. It's just people helping people. That's what relationships are all about."

"I'm beginning to think that's what life is about. Linda is an amazing lady and is becoming a close friend. I'm not sure she needs to learn how to **S.M.I.L.E.** since her business is doing so well. But she knows a lot of business people, so I thought I'd put you two together."

"I look forward to us getting together, which I assure you would put a smile on my face. Speaking of getting together, I dropped by to see if you and Doug could get together with Gwen and me this Friday evening for a little celebration. I promised once you learned how to **S.M.I.L.E.** that I'd make that happen."

Sherri's reaction went from jubilation . . . to disbelief. "Can we make it any day other than this Friday? I've accepted an invitation to the Carters' party that evening, and I promised I'd be there. Plus, I think Doug has something going on Friday too. What about during the week or even Saturday? Please tell me one of those days is available!"

Rolly mirrored her disappointment. "I'm sorry, but we have guests for the week, and then we leave on Sunday for a vacation in the Caribbean to visit family."

"Bummer!" Sherri responded. "Not a bummer that you've got company or are taking a vacation. I'm excited for you. I'm just disappointed I'll have to wait even longer to introduce you to Doug and his team."

"When it's supposed to happen, it will happen," Rolly reassured her. "Would it cheer you up to tell me about your recent successes? Let's begin with your visit to Christophe's neighborhood. I hear the two of you got to enjoy your time in his playground with a couple who walked in."

Rolly's invitation was a welcome diversion. Escorting him inside for Goldfish and water, Sherri went on and on about Christophe's execution of **S.M.I.L.E.** Rolly smiled as she chronicled Christophe's use of the checklist to help a couple looking to build a new home make the little decisions that led them to a purchase. "It was as smooth as the butter he spread on my English muffin that morning," she remarked.

Rolly chuckled at her comparison. She then shared that the couple owned a home they wanted to sell, so she accepted an invitation to follow them to their residence. In no time, they were saying yes to the checklist of little decisions that resulted in a listing.

The day culminated with Christophe and Priscilla joining her and Doug, along with Christophe and Sherri's newest Ambassadors, for a celebration dinner. "Our favorite waiter, Rob Lee, made us *all* feel like royalty!" she proclaimed.

"Nicely done! An after-hours get-together really solidifies the relationship," Rolly said. "Christophe told me the rest of your weekend was pretty special too."

A First Time for Everything

She began sharing a remarkable experience regarding a call she took on phone duty Saturday morning. "Holding myself acCOUNTable to applying everything I learned about S.M.I.L.E., I made a conscious decision to enjoy everyone I meet and everything I do."

"The *E* in S.M.I.L.E. is a great way to begin every day!" Rolly emphasized. "Personally *and* professionally."

"I agree. So a family called about a property they had driven by and wanted to see. I said I'd be happy to arrange that but suggested I could likely save them both time and effort if we first met to get a better feel for their situation. We agreed on brunch at a quaint restaurant nearby."

"A change of scenery at a better 'candy store.' Bob and Sarah would agree."

"It worked! I began by focusing on the signs I pretended

they were wearing, and the couple agreed to mute their phones while we visited. Within minutes, I identified the wife as an Owl, which meant I had to be very detailed with her. The husband was a Parrot, so I knew I needed to keep it fun for him."

"The *I* in **S.M.I.L.E.** Susan would applaud you."

"My goal was to make this simple for me and for them. When they eventually brought up the home they had driven by and were interested in seeing, I shifted the conversation to what they HAVE NOW. Using my notepad, I divided the page into the four areas. By the time we had filled it out, we all had a much better understanding of their situation. Then once we completed the second page addressing what they were LOOKING FOR, we realized the home they had called about didn't work. They agreed our getting together first was very beneficial."

"The *S* in **S.M.I.L.E.** Bob and Sarah would be proud."

"Next, I brought in the engaging question Christophe shared—whether they had ever purchased or built a home before, even though they had already volunteered they were currently leasing."

"Sherri, I'm pleased you realize that the question must be asked. Whether they own or rent, have ever bought or not, have ever built or not, each sets up the opportunity to explain the little decisions."

"Precisely! So when they said no, I simply shared that the decision to buy a home is not one big decision but a series of little decisions. Then I began writing those little decisions on paper.

"When I asked where they would like to begin, their priorities centered on their boys. To the wife, the quality of the schools was paramount, narrowing our search to one school district that met their requirements. The husband was most interested in the homesite, a property with a big backyard for the boys to practice baseball and soccer. He proudly shared he would be coaching them in their youth programs."

"How commendable on both their parts. They sound like great parents."

"They are and I complimented them on that. Now here's the best part, Rolly. Getting that specific narrowed our search to only three properties."

"Returning to the *S* in **S.M.I.L.E.**, fewer jars of jam."

"Yes. And by the time we placed checkmarks beside the schools and the homesite, as well as the home and neighborhood, their need to buy became quite obvious."

"The power of the *L* in **S.M.I.L.E.** So . . . ?"

"So . . . they bought! We presented their offer that evening, and it was accepted this morning."

"I'm so proud of you! Were you surprised?"

"As it was happening, yes. But looking back, no. I held myself acCOUNTable to be willing to **S.M.I.L.E.**, and I got lucky! Then when I dropped off the signed copies of the agreement, along with four tickets to a local minor league baseball game, I got even luckier. Before I could ask, they referred a coworker from the husband's company and offered to give me a Quality Introduction."

"I'm thrilled for you! And the baseball tickets were a nice touch. I'll bet the boys were on cloud nine."

"Everyone was. It reminded me of the feeling I had giving out stars to my students. I'm making a difference again. And I love how different that feels."

"I'm glad, Sherri. And your turning ME into WE with

the referral completes the last of the letters. Congratulations! You've mastered **S.M.I.L.E.** in only two weeks. Our next step is to get you involved in teaching it to others. That is, if you're still interested."

"More than anything! But even more than that, I would love to learn who referred *me* to you. I've been thinking about it and I'm convinced it's Charlene. We talk every day, and she's been super interested in how I'm doing. It's her, isn't it?"

"That, my dear, will be revealed sooner than you think. For now, let me get with my team to see who could use your assistance," Rolly suggested, heading toward the door.

"Please tell them I said hello. May I get the door for you? It would be my pleasure."

"I've heard it takes twenty-one days to create a new habit," he said. "I believe you've done it in fourteen!"

"I told you I was a quick learner. Now give me a hug so I can go talk to Charlene. I plan to get a confession out of her."

"Good luck with that. Oh, and enjoy your party with the Carters," he hollered as he flew away.

A Celebration

We are so glad you could make it, Sherri!" Linda said, offering a warm hug and a smile.

"Thank you. I'm honored to be here. Please forgive me for being late. I couldn't explain the details in the message I left you, but a family wanted to revisit the first property we viewed today before we wrote a purchase agreement. They're first-time home buyers and needed to feel certain it was the right home."

"You showed the same compassion for us. At times a little

hand holding and reassurance are all that's needed. Dave is out back with everyone. We'll head there in a sec. Let me take your jacket and . . . what do you have here?"

"A bottle of your favorite wine. You said no gifts, but I thought if we enjoyed a glass together, you'd be okay with it."

"You are so considerate, which is one of the reasons why we asked you to join us tonight. This is a special occasion and our way of saying thanks."

"I feel special just being invited. You mentioned there were business owners you wanted me to meet?"

"Yes, but there's an even bigger reason you're here. We have a special surprise—a celebration that will put a smile on a lot of faces."

"I love celebrations . . . and smiles! What's it for?"

"You're about to find out. First, I need you to close your eyes. Excellent, and keep them closed. Okay, hold out your arms so I can slip this around your shoulders . . . like . . . this. And this goes on your head . . . like . . . so."

Sherri felt the weight of what she imagined must be some sort of sheet or cape around her shoulders. In addition, what seemed to be a bunch of loose strings from the hat would brush her forehead whenever she moved her head.

"You look great!" Linda said. "Now, just hold my hand as we step outside, and don't open your eyes until you're told."

Entering the backyard, Sherri was greeted by a familiar voice that came from in front of her and Linda. "You can open your eyes and smile for everyone!"

Seeing Rolly perched at the far end of a banquet table, Sherri stood in shock as everyone applauded. Tears filled her eyes. Then she rushed toward Rolly as he did her. And when the two embraced, the guests cheered. "What are you doing here?" she asked.

"Well, you're donning a graduation cap and gown," Rolly pointed out. "We're here to honor your successful completion of **S.M.I.L.E.** Congratulations on that *and* on the sale you just made, which *made* us wait forty-five minutes to kick this thing off."

"Surely Linda told you what happened. You know I'm never late."

"Surely you know I'm kidding. Before we begin the official ceremony, you might want to say hello to everyone. You'll see some familiar faces and some new ones. There's my lovely wife over there. Gwen can't wait to meet you. But I know you'll want to first thank the Carters for making all this happen for you!"

With tears still flowing, Sherri hugged Linda and Dave like never before. "So you're the 'someone I know and trust, someone who really believes in me and wants me to be success-ful.' *Finally* I get to thank you for changing my life, personally and professionally!"

"You are so deserving!" Linda said, also in tears.

"I feel blessed. And when I look back, it all makes sense now," Sherri said, shaking her head in disbelief. "Both times Rolly showed up at my home, I had just gotten off the phone with you. How could I not have put two and two together?"

"Because you were too busy trying to pin it on me," Char-lene replied.

Sherri could not believe her ears. "Charlene! You know Linda . . . and Rolly, too?"

"How do you think my salon business has grown so much? I've also learned to **S.M.I.L.E.**"

"So all the conversations . . . all the interest you've shown, you understood what I was experiencing."

"Keeping that secret was the hardest thing I've ever done. You know how hairdressers like to talk, especially one who's a Parrot!"

"I knew you were a Parrot the minute Susan described that behavioral style, and I told her so."

"Yes, you did, and why don't you say hello to the lady who taught you that," Susan interjected.

"Oh my goodness!" Sherri exclaimed, offering Susan a hug. "This is like a reunion. Thank you for coming tonight. But most of all thank you for teaching me about behavioral styles. I use that knowledge every day with every person I meet. Now I understand why you said it forever changed your real estate career. It's having the same effect on mine. And I'm just loving life and having fun."

"Fun? Sounds like my cue to step in," Bert remarked. "I wanted to greet my two favorite huggers at the same time!"

"Well, we can make that happen," Susan responded as she and Sherri embraced him together.

Bert grinned. "I think I'm enjoying this celebration more than you, Sherri."

"I'm enjoying not working a day since I met you and Ariff. Is he going to surprise me next?"

"Ariff would have given anything to be here, but his schedule was too tight. Oh! He did ask me to show you this." Bert scrolled through his phone for a photo Ariff had sent. "Check this out. He loved your comment about Mr. Rogers so much that he bought a zip-up cardigan."

"Going from a business suit to a sweater was probably not

easy. Maybe he's getting comfortable being uncomfortable. Tell Ariff I like his more casual look."

"If you like casual, I should have worn my overalls. I garden best in them!" Bob interjected. "And you may not recognize me without a bucket of tomatoes."

"Bob!" Sherri cried, giving him the sincerest of hugs. "Of course I recognize you! You are so thoughtful to come. Is Carolyn here too?"

"She isn't, but she didn't want me to come alone. So turn around and meet Sarah *in person.*"

"Oh my," Sherri gasped, her eyes welling up again. "Let me give you a hug!"

"It's so nice to meet you face-to-face," Sarah said. "I brought you a little something to remember me by."

Sherri opened the bag Sarah handed her. "Candy! How appropriate. I can't begin to tell you the difference that has made. The family I helped today agreed to meet for a late breakfast at the cutest little diner. By the time we left, we had fewer jars of jam to consider in the way of homes than we had choices of jam for breakfast! And I have you and Bob to thank for that."

"I'm so glad we could help. And let me help you by holding the candy for you. You've still got a lot of hugs to give. Rolly has kept us informed on how well you're doing."

"I feel like a kid again. I really do! That reminds me, Sarah, how are your little ones? I'd love to meet them. Or better yet, bring them over some night so Doug and I can babysit. We *pay* fifteen dollars an hour!"

"I think we could up that to twenty bucks for Sarah's two. I've met them. They are darling!" Doug exclaimed.

Sherri's eyes widened. "Darling . . . Doug . . . what are you doing here?" she asked in shock.

"Your Eagle has landed," Doug replied with a kiss and the most loving embrace.

"So you know Rolly! And your team knows how to **S.M.I.L.E.!** No wonder your sales have increased. No wonder Cody offered to give me Quality Introductions. Why didn't you tell me, you rascal?"

"For the same reason you didn't tell me. How could I explain that a parrot flew into my office to teach my team how to **S.M.I.L.E.?** Would you have believed it?"

"Probably not. So who referred Rolly to you?"

"We did," Linda spoke up.

"Oh my! You and Dave have been busy," Sherri remarked. "But you knew me first. You bought your home months before you purchased your new car."

"Yes, but we actually started looking for a car first. We postponed buying one until we closed on our home so the car payment wouldn't count against us."

"Now it's all coming together. So you and Dave referred Rolly to Doug *and* me. And is it safe to say you referred all the business owners who are here tonight to Rolly as well?"

"Our fair share," Linda modestly responded with a nod. "As I recall, Rolly met Charlie and Harry Roberts on his own. I didn't introduce him to Joe Brown or Camille White either."

Sherri scanned the crowd with excitement. "So are *all* of them here?"

Linda pointed to a large group standing near the pool. "They're right over there beside that beautiful garden sculpture you gave us. Oh, the tall gentleman standing next to them is

Keith Zars, who built our pool. And the couple next to him is Stacy and Melissa Grant, the owners of Crescent House Furniture. The unique furniture and accessory pieces you see came from them. Everyone is so excited to meet you and receive their Quality Introduction!"

"I'm honored and humbled and excited to meet all of them! But I must ask, how did *you* and Dave meet Rolly?"

James spoke up, "Since we're talking about the *M* in **S.M.I.L.E.**, I'll answer that."

Sherri smiled. "I was hoping I would see you. It means everything to me that you're here," she said as she hugged him. "I think it would mean a lot to John, too."

"I agree. So did you know Rolly actually taught Linda how to **S.M.I.L.E.** before any of us?"

"No, but that explains why her company has done so well," Sherri replied.

James agreed. "So to answer your question, Rolly was referred to Linda by her best friend, Susan Foer, who has known Rolly for some time. Susan's waving at us from right over there.

"Susan worked part-time for Linda and saw the value in getting them together. It goes back to our toast—it's all about relationships."

"It truly is!"

"And if I may intercept, those relationships will bring you more people than you can shake a stick at," Christophe stated.

"My personal chef! The man who made me queen for a day," Sherri said, greeting him with a hug. "By the way, it's inter*ject*, not inter*cept*."

"I always learn something new every time I see you. You're the best, Sherri!"

"Actually, you are—and your checklist! It has made the decision to buy or list a home so much easier for my guests. How can I ever thank you, Christophe? How can I thank *all* of you who have taught me how to **S.M.I.L.E.**?"

"You already have," Christophe responded as James handed him a specially designed thank-you card as tall as Rolly. "Sherri, you were so gracious in sending each of us a personal thank-you note, along with a gift certificate, so we created a card just for you. Oh, and we included a little something special for you and Doug. We hope you enjoy your trip."

"Enjoy our trip?" Sherri asked, sounding bewildered. Inside the card was an envelope with two round-trip tickets to Washington, D.C.

Rolly spoke up. "Because Doug chose not to be at the taping with Bert and Ariff—so he could surprise you here—and since Ariff couldn't make your celebration, we thought we'd send both of you to our nation's capital next month to continue your celebration, as well as Doug's. It was Ariff's idea. He wants to get a picture of both of you with him in his new cardigan."

Sherri was clearly touched by the thoughtfulness and generosity. Doug put his arm around her and nodded his approval. "I guess this Dove and her Eagle will be taking flight very soon!" she said with anticipation. "Thank you all so much! We can't wait to continue our celebration!"

"Right now we need to conclude this one," Rolly replied. "So are you ready for your ceremony?"

"You bet! Let's wrap this up so I can meet all these fine people. That way, this evening isn't all about *me*. I want to be able to help *them*!"

"You deserve to be in the spotlight, little Dove, whether you like it or not," Christophe said. "You've learned to **S.M.I.L.E.** faster than anyone ever! You even beat Doug's team, which started before you. Because of scheduling issues with a large group, they won't finish until next week."

"So when is their graduation, and do I get to attend?" Sherri asked Linda.

"Graduation is set for two weeks from tonight, when Rolly is back from vacation and just before you and Doug leave on your trip. And without question, you're invited!"

Sherri jumped up and down like a schoolgirl. Then she turned to Rolly. "So *part* of what you told me was true. You *are* taking a trip."

"*Everything* I told you was true. When you wanted to introduce me to Linda, I said it sounds like we need to get together. Remember? And when I invited you and Doug to join Gwen and me for a little celebration tonight, isn't that what we're doing? I just didn't tell you where and with whom."

"You're sneaky!" she replied, wagging her finger.

"Oh, I always have something up my sleeve."

"How can you do that, Rolly?" Christophe asked. "You're not wearing a shirt."

Everyone chuckled. "Let's get this party started," Linda suggested. "May I have everyone's attention? I've asked Rolly to do the honors. My dearest friend, they're yours."

"Thank you, Linda, for the privilege," Rolly responded with a respectful bow. Then turning toward the crowd, he spoke from his heart. "This evening is a celebration . . . of both accomplishments *and* acknowledgments. Throughout this journey, Sherri has humbly given credit for her success to everyone who has helped her along the way. And we feel privileged to have made a contribution. But now it's time to acknowledge where the credit truly belongs—to someone who chose to make a commitment that led to those accomplishments! Sherri, would you hold up your hands and wiggle your fingers?"

Blushing from the attention, she raised her hands. "Boy, am I glad I got my nails done this morning!"

All enjoyed a good laugh. Then Rolly continued. "Sherri held herself acCOUNTable, and we are so proud of her success. Without commitment, without accountability, nothing happens. Now we're hoping we can count on her to help share **S.M.I.L.E.** with others. Sherri, will you accept this new challenge?"

"Speech! Speech! Speech!" everyone chanted.

Sherri struggled to fight back tears. "Rolly, when you first introduced it, I thought **S.M.I.L.E.** was about putting a smile on *my* face. How wrong I was. It's not that at all. **S.M.I.L.E.** is about putting a smile on everyone *else's* face! And just look at all the smiles here tonight."

The crowd cheered!

Motioning Rolly to her side, she addressed him directly. "It's been a *joyous* journey. And this journey of **S.M.I.L.E.** has me smiling more than ever. I loved learning it. I will love teaching it. But most of all . . . I love living it! Rolly, I humbly and proudly accept your invitation." She then turned to address everyone. "Now this Dove is done talking. It's time to begin building the relationships with all you extraordinary people so, together, *we* can help put a smile on even more faces!"

"Our Dove is turning into an Eagle," Rolly answered. "In no time, she'll have the whole world smiling!"

Everyone erupted in celebration!

Acknowledgments

"Everyone I meet is here to teach me something."
—Steve Rigby

Because everyone I've met *has* taught me something—regardless of how large or how small—then it would only by fitting that thanks must be given to everyone I know or have known. So . . . thank you to all who have crossed my path!

Since some contributions have been a little larger than others, I wish to give specific thanks to the following . . .

Doug Stempowski, who introduced me to Rolly Stirman—*the* Rolly in *S.M.I.L.E.* Both men were gracious in taking me under their wings during my early years in sales, sales management, and training. I would not be where I am today without their help and guidance.

Rick Andreen, a rookie on my sales team, who inspired me to start reading again. Rick gave me *The 7 Habits of Highly Effective People*, the first business book I read during my extended college break. Though I thought I was done learning, that book taught me that I still had an awful lot to learn. As a result, I've read hundreds upon hundreds of business books ever since. In all likelihood, I would never have become an author without that very first book. What a gift that book was. What a gift Rick was!

Dr. Stephen Covey, author of *The 7 Habits of Highly*

Effective People, whom I had the honor of joining for lunch one day. Over our meal, he challenged me, "Steve, if you want to live *The Seven Habits,* you must *teach* the habits." I refer to them with *every* class I've ever conducted. That original copy is worn and tattered beyond its years, with the binding long since gone. I think Dr. Covey would be proud of how ragged it looks and to know that I heeded his advice. Thank you, Dr. Covey!

Ken Blanchard and Andy Andrews, who I've also had the privilege of meeting. Both have inspired me with their creativity and writing styles. It was their books that prompted the idea of a most unusual character to carry the story line of *S.M.I.L.E.* The fables and fun and enlightening stories in their books captured my attention. You know you're reading a great book when you can't put it down. I could never put theirs down! Thanks for all the inspiring stories you've shared with the world!

Karen Langdon, who helped with the early stages of editing *S.M.I.L.E.* as the story was still unfolding. Her positive encouragement kept me going.

B. J. Brown, who took over the "heavy lifting" of editing *S.M.I.L.E.* She burned the midnight oil far too many nights. The praise my publisher reaped on the quality of the manuscript it was given is bestowed upon B. J. She is a master at putting thoughts on a blank page. You are a blessing.

Dewitt Jones, who honored me by writing the Foreword for *S.M.I.L.E.* As a premiere photojournalist for *National Geographic,* Dewitt's videos about photography, and his stories about life from his years with *National Geographic,* have moved me beyond words. These pieces are the bookends for *all* my Retreats. His messages of purpose and passion, of vision and values, of patience and persistence, of creativity and caring, of changing your lens to change your life, and of celebrating what's right with the world have been the mainstay for my journey. Thanks for being a trusted friend and mentor. I cherish our relationship.

Lilla Cummings, for her wonderful photo for the jacket. I am in awe of her ability to capture the right feeling in a photograph that says more than words could ever express.

The Greenleaf Book Group team: Tanya Hall, Danny Sandoval, Daniel Pederson, Jessica Choi, Olivia McCoy, Sam Alexander, Corrin Foster, Kristine Peyre-Ferry, Sheila Parr, Teresa Muniz, Judy Marchman, Kirstin Andrews, Claire Jentsch, Carrie Jones, Tyler LeBleu, Stephanie Mlynarski, AprilJo Murphy, Chelsea Richards, Dylan Ross, Chantel Stull, Sujan Trivedi, Brian Viktorin, Shannon Zuniga, Sam Alexander, Tiffany Barrientos, Sophie Brame, Justin Branch, Rachael Brandenburg, Gardiner Brown, Bethany Chapoy, Lindsey Clark, Nathan DeLacretaz, Steven Elizalde, Sally Garland, Jen Glynn, and Neil Gonzalez. All of you have been the absolute best to work with! You make me smile!

Scott James for his branding efforts with *S.M.I.L.E.* And for being the best "typewriter poet" ever!

Sarah Wilson, our publicist, for her extraordinary talent of spreading the message of *S.M.I.L.E.* Your energy is contagious!

Everyone who played a part in *S.M.I.L.E.* Not only did they earn a place in my book, they will forever hold a place in my heart. You can learn more about each of them at **www.stevemrigby.com**. They're the best.

To all my friends, my ambassadors, who have helped spread the message of *S.M.I.L.E.* You'll never know how deeply I appreciate your help!

Lastly, I pay tribute to my family. My grandfather, Travis Bracewell. He taught me the value in putting people first. My parents, E. C. and Bobbie Rigby. In the words of my songwriting brother, Richard Leigh, "Everything they gave, took all they had." My siblings: David, Laura, Paul, and Lynda. I did my best to be a good brother. My children: Tammy, Tracy, Clint, Courtney, Brock, and Brooke. I did my best to be a loving and caring father. My grandchildren: Elizabeth, Melody, and Kaitlyn. I'm doing my best to spoil them. My bride, Susan. I'm doing my best to be the man she deserves.

Resources for S.M.I.L.E.

S.M.I.L.E.

SIMPLE . . . for me
. . . for my guests

ME  *into* **WE**

Identify the
*I*ndividual

LITTLE *decisions simplify
the bigger ones!*

ENJOY *everyone and
everything*

Seven Rules of Shopping

1st: We're just big kids . . . with more money.

2nd: We prefer to buy from people we trust.

3rd: We can be influenced by someone
who listens.

4th: We don't argue with our own answers.

5th: Little decisions help simplify the
bigger ones.

6th: Until we buy, our situation has
not improved.

7th: We will tell others about our experience.

Accountability Lists

Day 1

- [ ] Have more fun.

- [ ] Use manners.

- [ ] Set phone to "Respectful" while with others.

- [ ] Notice things.

- [ ] Make the other person feel important.

- [ ] Put people first and product second.

- [ ] Offer hugs.

- [ ] Hold myself acCOUNTable.

- [ ] Replace "no problem" with "my pleasure."

- [ ] Always wear a smile.

- [ ] The most important sale I will make is me!

- [ ] Focusing on my purpose will help keep it SIMPLE . . . for me!

Day 2

- ☐ Let character be my guide.

- ☐ Being present is the greatest gift you can give.

- ☐ Limit the number of "jams."

- ☐ Learn what they LIKE, DISLIKE, and would like to CHANGE about what they HAVE NOW.

- ☐ Discover what they're LOOKING FOR, along with what they WANT and what they NEED.

- ☐ Write their answers down!

- ☐ Make a business decision based on my time.

- ☐ Change the scenery. Find a better "candy store."

Day 3

☐ *If I want to S.M.I.LE., it's up to ME. Smart sales people build relationships.*

☐ *I will build my business on referrals by getting into the people business!*

☐ *It's up to ME to turn . . .*

☐ *Remembering special occasions helps build relationships.*

☐ *Staying in touch helps maintain the relationships.*

Day 4

- [ ] Look for the clues of how others see the world.
- [ ] Adjust my style to make others feel comfortable.

Day 5

- [ ] Enjoy everyone . . . and everything!
- [ ] Love what you do, and you can retire today!
- [ ] Practicing the P Paradox ensures I will enjoy everyone and everything!

Day 6

- [ ] Little is BIG!
- [ ] A checklist—on paper—is the key.
- [ ] Circle their answers! Focus on one at a time!
- [ ] YES is their answer to a better future.

Photograph by Lilla Cummings Photography

About the Author

For nearly two decades, Steve Rigby served the homebuilding industry as both a student and a teacher of selling, managing, and training. He was responsible for directing the sales efforts for three of the nation's top-ten public homebuilders. As a result, those companies experienced tremendous growth with very healthy bottom lines.

In the past decade plus, Steve has continued to prove his proficiency as a thought leader through his own business, New Wings Consulting, LLC, which serves companies across a variety of industries. As he's accustomed to seeing, those companies are also experiencing tremendous growth and very healthy bottom lines.

Steve resides on Lake Travis, just outside Austin, Texas,

with his wife, Susan, their two horses, Blondie and Envy, and their dog, Drizzle.

If you're up for a visit, he and Susan conduct retreats at their cabin on the lake. Those who have been there will tell you it's something worth considering!